BASEBALL IN THE LONE STAR STATE

Baseball
in the
LONE STAR STATE

THE TEXAS LEAGUE'S GREATEST HITS

TOM KAYSER *and* DAVID KING

TRINITY UNIVERSITY PRESS

San Antonio

Published by Trinity University Press
San Antonio, Texas 78212

Copyright © 2005 by Tom Kayser and David King

Cover design by Pentagram, Austin
Book design by BookMatters, Berkeley

⊛ The paper used in this publication meets the minimum
requirements of the American National Standard for
Information Sciences-Permanence of Paper for Printed
Library Materials, ANSI Z39.48-1992.

For a complete list of sources and further reading,
please go to www.texasleague.com/history/research/

LIBRARY OF CONGRESS CATALOGING-IN-PUBLICATION DATA

Kayser, Tom.
   Lone star state : the Texas League's greatest hits /
Tom Kayser and David King.
      p.   cm.
"Episodic chapters tell the history of the Texas League,
   providing a broad picture of the shifting character of
   baseball operations in this minor league over the past
   century. Black and white photos and an appendix of
   baseball statistics are included" —Provided by publisher.
   ISBN 1-59534-012-2 (hardcover : alk. paper)—
   ISBN 1-59534-013-0 (pbk. : alk. paper)
   1. Texas League—History.   2. Texas League—
Statistics.   3. Minor league baseball—Texas—History.
I. King, David, 1958–   II. Title.
GV875.T36K39   2005
796.357'64'09764--dc22   2004029741

Printed in the United States of America
09   08   07   06   05 — 5   4   3   2   1

CONTENTS

THIRD BASE: STRUGGLE TO SURVIVE

HOME: A REVIVAL

Photograph section follows page 116.

PREFACE

The idea for a book about some of the great stories of the Texas League can be traced to one of my visits to Tom Kayser's house. After seeing the house—which also serves as the office of the Texas League, repository of hundreds of pages of information, and a museum of baseball history—I suggested that someday, "somebody" ought to compile some of this stuff into a book. "Oh sure," Tom said, not taking the hint, "I'll get around to it."

Finally, in the spring of 2003, Tom called and said he had been talking to Char Miller and Barbara Ras at Trinity University Press about all the historical information he had collected on the league. He said that they were enthusiastic about finally turning all these fascinating stories into a book, and apparently he had taken the hint that I wanted to write it (this was not long after I finished *San Antonio at Bat*, a history of professional baseball in San Antonio). The meeting was set, but the significance of the location didn't really click for me until I arrived. When we sat down to lunch, we had a view of the site of one of San Antonio's most noteworthy ballparks, League Park. Of course, League Park had burned to the ground in the 1930s, nearly taking the entire neighborhood with it. Today, an industrial complex occupies the site and a freeway runs through where the outfield would have been. But we took it as a good sign.

Perhaps the toughest part of the project was deciding which stories to include. Since the Texas League began play in 1888, thousands of games have been played by thousands of players in forty different cities, from New Mexico to Mississippi. Choosing the highlights was tough.

Fortunately, Tom is a dedicated list maker—lists seem to be everywhere in his office—and we were able to pare down the hundreds of ideas to a manageable number. We made some of the decisions on a practical basis—there just wasn't enough information on some of the people, places, or games available to do them justice. In most cases that wasn't a problem, though, because after years of dedicated sleuthing through libraries from one end of the league to the other, Tom has been able to document just about anything of note in the league's history with at least one, and usually multiple, newspaper or magazine reports.

The compiling of the photos was a different story, for though the Texas League library is extensive, there were significant gaps. Part of the problem was that Tom has only been in charge of the league—and collecting photos—since 1992. Once our needs were identified, we were able to collect, beg, borrow, and in some cases buy the photos that illustrate the stories in the book.

Our roles were decidedly different with *Texas League*. Tom had already done virtually all the heavy lifting, compiling the information from newspapers and magazines and books past and present into neat files. My job was to bring them to life in relatively short chapters that could be read in sequence or at random. He would then read each chapter and edit, making suggestions and tossing in additional facts.

After months of struggle—and many trips by Tom's house to pick up and drop off files—the book finally wrapped up during one long weekend at the end of March. I was in St. Louis covering a National Collegiate Athletic Association men's basketball regional, writing like a madman when I wasn't working at my regular job, and Tom was editing furiously amid all his duties as the president of the league, with opening day rapidly approaching. The entire process of research, writing, and editing went surprisingly smoothly, perhaps because we are both deadline-oriented and able to corral our egos. That or we just wanted to get the thing done.

We want to thank the people at Trinity University Press for taking a chance on this project, as well as all the librarians, archivists, and baseball historians who have helped compile this information through the years.

David King and Tom Kayser

INTRODUCTION

JUST AS THE CIVIL WAR WAS A TURNING POINT IN THE political life of the United States, so was it for the game of baseball. The mixing of soldiers from different regions of the country—east and west, north and south—allowed the game of "base" to spread across the growing nation. Young men returning to their homes from the war began to play contests on weekends and holidays. Fans lined rough-hewn fields to watch.

Those spectators piqued the interest of a group of businessmen, who in 1871 formed the National Association, the first professional baseball league, and in 1876 the National League, to play games for fans in the nation's largest cities.

The league was successful enough to spawn imitators, including one formed by a group led by Arthur "Candy" Cummings. The group met in Pittsburgh in the winter of 1876 and founded the International Association, figuring that if people in the big cities would pay to see baseball, so would people in smaller communities. The International Association, made up of eight teams from Canada and the northern United States, played a twenty-game schedule in 1877.

More leagues began popping up, especially in the rapidly industrializing North and Midwest, where people were earning enough money to afford leisure activities. The League Alliance and the Northwestern League soon followed the other new leagues.

The spread of new leagues continued in the next decade. One league that sprang up in the Midwest, the Western League, included a team in St. Joseph, Missouri, that counted on its roster a marginally talented but extremely bright young man from Louisville named John McCloskey. When the 1887 season ended, McCloskey put together a league all-star team—dubbed the Joplin Independents—that he planned to take to the West Coast to continue playing throughout most of the winter. To stay sharp, McCloskey's team scheduled contests against local squads along the way, including those in Fort Worth, Waco, and Austin.

The Independents beat the Fort Worth and Waco teams handily. In Austin, a tip from a friendly bellman at his hotel let McCloskey know what was up: a couple of local businessmen had brought in a team of ringers, many from a league called the Southern Association. McCloskey's Independents managed to beat the ringers. But more important, he recognized that anyone willing to go to those lengths to beat a touring team might be interested in staging baseball full-time. He met with the two Austinites, Sam French and Ed Byrne, and got the concept of a Texas-based league rolling. By January, there were enough teams to field a league.

But as with any new business, there were going to be pitfalls. The weather could be a problem because, with field maintenance rudimentary at best, rain could knock out several games. No one, not even McCloskey, knew exactly how much money it was going to take to operate a ball club. Most of the owners had no idea how to recruit and sign ballplayers. Still, on April 1, 1888, the first Texas League of Base Ball Clubs game was played in Houston, and the remainder of the league started play soon thereafter. But it wasn't long before the teams began to struggle. San Antonio, with a team made up of local amateurs, dropped out in June, followed soon afterward by Fort Worth. By July every remaining club was reporting financial problems.

In one form or another, though, the league played on through September, and it managed to stay afloat for two more years before failing finances killed it. McCloskey came back to reorganize it for 1892, but it lasted just one season. Businessman Ted Sullivan helped revive it again in 1895, and it continued through 1899 before financial problems once again overwhelmed its owners.

Of course, the Texas League was not the only league struggling through the final years of the nineteenth century; leagues came and went with regularity. But the Texas League was fortunate in having McCloskey and a small but dedicated group of businessmen who between them kept the league bouncing back. It came back for good in 1902, a season that featured one of its greatest teams, the Corsicana Oil City.

The Oilers were the first—but certainly not the only—Texas League team to benefit from the discovery of oil in the state. A nation that was rapidly becoming industrialized needed power, and oil was an ideal way to produce it. The booming east Texas oilfields pumped money into the entire state, and that money was one of the major reasons the Texas League survived when so many others failed.

After that, even a split between north and south Texas couldn't kill the league. After four seasons with both a North Texas League and a South Texas League, the owners got together in 1907 and united the regions into an eight-team loop that included the cities that would be the foundation for the league through the next fifty years: Houston, Dallas, Fort Worth, and San Antonio. Other cities, from Waco to Austin to Galveston, came and went. Sometimes out-of-state teams were added, including longtime members Oklahoma City, Shreveport, and Tulsa. But it was Houston, the base of the oil boom; Dallas, the financial center;

Fort Worth, the gateway to the West; and old San Antonio, a growing center for commerce, that kept the Texas League diversified financially and solid as an organization.

Baseball began another boom era in the years after World War I, fueled in part by the abolition of a number of trick pitches (including the spitball) and the use of greater numbers of fresh (and what some claimed to be livelier) balls in games. Hitting soared through the 1920s, and not even the dominance of the Fort Worth Cats—who won every pennant from 1920 to 1925—could reduce enthusiasm for the game in Texas. An oil boom boosted Wichita Falls into the league's elite in the late 1920s, but by then another factor was starting to change the game.

During the 1920s, the St. Louis Cardinals—led by baseball pioneer Branch Rickey—began buying minor-league teams and using them to try out and develop hundreds of players from coast to coast. In the past, most minor-leaguers had been signed by the local owners, who had the final say on personnel matters. The relationships between the club owners and the big-league organizations had been on a personal level: San Antonio owner Harry Benson, for example, was friends with New York Giants manager John McGraw, and in 1923 McGraw sent Ike Boone to San Antonio. Boone led the league in hitting, at .402.

But the Cardinals began to flourish under Rickey's formula, developing players like Dizzy Dean, who played for the Cardinals' team in the Texas League, the Houston Buffs, in 1931. Other big-league clubs caught on to the idea. Some, like the St. Louis Browns, bought teams outright (San Antonio began a long affiliation with the Browns in 1933), while others, like the Detroit Tigers, formed player-sharing relationships (at first with Fort Worth, and then with Beaumont).

Even with the advent of Rickey's farm system, Texas League teams were still operated with a large degree of independence, and not all the players on the teams were signed by the parent team.

But with a degree of financial backing from the majors, the Texas League was able to survive the Depression, which winnowed out many of the leagues that had begun operations in the booming 1920s.

When World War II began, President Franklin D. Roosevelt urged the majors to continue playing games, but the minors received no such blessing. As the draft took more and more young men, all the leagues—major and minor—found it harder and harder to keep playing. Except for ten leagues, all minor leagues—including the Texas League—closed down for the duration (in the Texas League's case from 1943 to 1945).

However, the suspension of operations didn't kill the league. In fact, the postwar economic boom shot the minors to new heights in attendance. In 1949, the Texas League's eight teams drew just over 2 million fans, more than four times the number that saw contests in 1942. With the economy booming and fans flocking to the ballparks—some of them, like San Antonio's Mission Stadium, brand new—the league looked to be headed for more and more record years.

The postwar boom, however, turned out to be brief. Television, a technological marvel that had made a barely noticed debut before the war, became commercially viable. Every home could afford a set, and the programming was free. The previous technological innovation, the radio, had turned into a boon for baseball, building a fan base that followed the team on the air but still came out to the ballpark. (But even radio began to turn sour on the minors in the 1950s, as a loosening of restrictions allowed virtually unlimited broadcasts of big-league games all over the country, giving fans another reason to stay home.)

Television was another story. Its marvelous new pictures were more compelling than any radio play-by-play. It also brought the big leagues into every home in the country, so fans no longer had to watch the up-and-coming youngsters or the over-the-hill exbig-leaguers at the local park. They could watch Mickey Mantle and the New York Yankees, Jackie Robinson and the Brooklyn Dodgers, and Willie Mays and the New York Giants on television from the comfort of their homes.

Another piece of technology hurt baseball even further, especially in Texas: the air conditioner. The choice of entertainment no longer consisted only of sitting in the grandstand, waiting for the evening breezes to blow. Moviegoers were lured by refrigerated air, which eventually made its way into homes. Fewer and fewer fans wanted to go out to games and sit in the heat to watch minor-league baseball, which was seen as an inferior game and often treated that way by its big-league brethren.

The major leagues also sped up the minors' decline in the 1950s, moving teams into some of the best minor-league markets. Milwaukee, Baltimore, and Kansas City got big-league teams in the 1950s, and the Dodgers and Giants moved to the West Coast, taking over the two biggest cities there in 1958. Minneapolis–St. Paul and Houston were soon to follow when baseball began to expand. As a result, the number of minor leagues dropped precipitously. In 1951, there were fifty minor leagues scattered around North America, including six with at least one team in Texas. In 1959, there were twenty-one left, including a struggling Texas League.

The woes continued through much of the 1960s, hitting bottom in Texas when the National League's Houston Colt .45s, which owned the league's San Antonio franchise, moved it out of the city for Amarillo after the 1964 season. The Colts management blamed poor attendance and indifferent media coverage for the move. Many critics noted that the club had hurt itself by broadcasting Colts games on the San Antonio radio station that used to carry San Antonio games, and it made little effort to appeal to local fans to do anything but come to Houston for games.

Texas League attendance bottomed out at 589,952 in 1963, and it went up only slightly in the next few years even with the constant addition of new teams—Tulsa, El Paso, and Little Rock—and the return of Dallas–Fort Worth from Triple-A and San Antonio from oblivion. The league got to the point where it would try just about any market in its struggle to survive. Oil patch money got Midland into the league in 1972, as well as Alexandria, Louisiana. Midland's team survived even after the oil money began to dry up, but Alexandria's lasted just four seasons.

It took a revolution in marketing to finally get the Texas League headed upward again. Innovative team general managers Jim Paul in El Paso and Bill Valentine in Arkansas figured out that it was going to take more than just the game on the field to put people in the stands. They came up with giveaways (from balls to bats to caps) and wild events (a man who billed himself as "Captain Dynamite" created the illusion of blowing himself up in the middle of the infield) to attract people back to the ballparks, and they succeeded. During the 1970s, attendance around the league began to climb, led by El Paso and Arkansas.

A wave of nostalgia helped boost attendance at minor-league parks through the 1980s, as fans sought something a little more old-fashioned after seeing movies like *The Natural* and *Bull Durham*. A new set of standards mandated for minor-league stadiums helped spawn a building boom soon thereafter, with new stadiums going up in Shreveport, El Paso, and San Antonio in the late 1980s and early 1990s; several other stadiums got facelifts. Thanks to the shiny new ballparks filled with amenities for the fans, attendance continued to rise. And the values of franchises, which had sunk to five figures in the 1970s, soared into the millions.

The latest wave of change in the Texas League began in 1999, when former big-league pitcher Nolan Ryan and his business partners bought the Jackson Generals and announced they were moving the team to Round Rock, an Austin suburb. At least two attempts to build a stadium and bring the minors back to the Austin area had failed during the 1990s, but Ryan's name and financial clout were enough to make it happen. The Austin area rejoined the league in 2000 and immediately set league attendance records at Dell Diamond, the club's $25 million ballpark. (In its first season, Round Rock became the first Double-A team to top six hundred thousand in attendance). The team was marketed heavily in north Austin and the towns north of the city, which were populated by people in the booming high-tech sector. So instead of oil, the latest driving force in the league has been the silicon chip.

Two years later, the owners of the Shreveport club, seeing Ryan's success in the Austin area, moved their club to a new stadium in the Dallas suburb of Frisco. The team, marketed as a lower-cost alternative to the major leagues, played in a complex built by Tom Hicks, owner of the Texas Rangers and hockey's Dallas Stars. Frisco finished a close second to Round Rock in attendance, as both teams became part of a national trend that saw more and more minor-league teams move into big-league cities. Frisco topped 660,000 fans in its first season in the league.

Frisco and Round Rock are continuing the legacy of the Texas League, a legacy formed in economic upturns and built often by sheer force of will. The league has survived two world wars, a depression, and a twenty-year downturn, thanks in large part to changes that sometimes were a matter of sheer chance (like the end of the spitball, enforced from the majors) and sometimes were a matter of marketing skill (like the success of El Paso and Arkansas in the 1970s and Round Rock and Frisco in the 2000s).

But whether through luck, skill, or persistence, the Texas League has survived where hundreds of others have failed. And through more than one hundred summers, it has produced dozens of great teams, great players, and simply great stories.

=FIRST BASE=
THE EARLY DAYS

=1=
OPENING DAY

BASEBALL WAS A FAR DIFFERENT GAME IN 1888 THAN IT IS today. Then the pitcher stood just fifty feet from the plate in the "pitcher's point," a four-by-six-foot box. Without much in the way of protective gear, the catcher was often as far as forty feet from the plate. Many pitchers still threw underhanded, as had been the rule up until 1884, and they got five "wides," or balls, before a batter earned a walk. Fielders wore either small gloves that covered just their palms or no gloves at all.

But perhaps equally noteworthy in the early days of the game was what went on in the stands. A writer from the *Houston Daily Post* made this observation at the very first Texas League game ever played, between the Houston Babies and the Galveston Giants on April 1, 1888, at Houston's City Park: "A large crowd came over from Galveston to see the Giants do up the Babies. The visitors brought plenty of money with them, but every dollar they offered was promptly covered by Sam Alexander and other plucky Houstonians." Houston won that first game 4–1, sending the Galvestonians home unhappy and slightly lighter in the wallets, and the Texas League, the brainchild of John J. McCloskey and a group of young Texas businessmen, was born.

The first batter in the first game in league history was Houston catcher Danny Joe Murphy, who popped up to first baseman B. F. Sullivan. The first hit in league history was by Galveston second baseman Joe E. Dowie in the second inning, and Houston's Pat Flaherty scored the first run in the third. Mike Shea, who had pitched in two games for the Cincinnati Red Stockings in the American Association—at the time a major league—was the winning pitcher for Houston. Losing pitcher John Bates would go the opposite direction, appearing in a game for the American Association's Kansas City club in 1889.

And while the baseball-writing pun wasn't invented on April 2, 1888, the unidentified writer for the *Houston Daily Post* managed to toss in the first of what would be hundreds of thousands throughout the league's 100-plus seasons: "The game from post to finish was a close and exciting exhibition of good ball. But at the same time it was apparent to all after the second inning that the Babies were too lusty and too muscular to be spanked by the Giants."

=2=
JOHN McCLOSKEY

JOHN McCLOSKEY HAD AN EARLY AND ABIDING PASSION FOR baseball. He landed his first job in the game in 1876 as a fourteen-year-old batboy for a club in his hometown of Louisville, Kentucky, and for the next sixty-six years, he was involved in baseball as a player, manager, scout, executive, and, most important, as the founder of the Texas League.

McCloskey first came to Texas in 1884 as a catcher in a semipro league that had teams in Houston, Galveston, San Antonio, Fort Worth, and Dallas. Three and a half years later, he returned, this time leading a team of players from the Western League that was barnstorming its way from Missouri to California. His Joplin Independents played local squads in Fort Worth and Waco, and they had a date scheduled with a team from Austin.

In Austin, two businessmen, lumberman Sam French and contractor Ed Byrne, had put together a group they thought could knock off McCloskey's squad. "A friendly clerk in the hotel tipped me off to the fact that the Austin folk had gotten together the star players of the Southern League," McCloskey told Texas League historian William Ruggles in 1931. McCloskey's team won anyway, and he came away with the idea that baseball might just be a hit in Austin.

With two relatively wealthy partners and the promise of big crowds—the city was filling up for ceremonies to mark the opening of the state's new capitol building—the Independents issued a challenge to the National League's New York Giants, who were also barnstorming the state. McCloskey, French, and Byrne lined up a three-game series in Austin. "The Giants demanded a thousand dollars guarantee, with the winner to take 65 percent," McCloskey told Ruggles. "Byrne wired back that the offer was accepted but the winner would have to take 85 percent. "I was not especially confident, but we did have a good team." The Independents won the first two games of the series in front of good crowds, but the third game was canceled when the Giants quietly slipped out of town. (The fate of the guarantee was not reported.)

McCloskey stayed, though, and began to stir up interest in a professional baseball league in the state. A meeting in December brought together business leaders from Austin, Houston, Dallas, and New Orleans, who began to organize a league that would begin play in April 1888. Another meeting in January clarified the league's composition—New Orleans had bolted to the Southern League, but Galveston, Fort Worth, and San Antonio were added to the newly named Texas League of Base Ball Clubs.

McCloskey's Independents became Austin's team, and the first Texas League season opened on April 1, 1888. Eschewing a leadership role in the league as he would through much of his career, McCloskey played center field for Austin on opening day against San Antonio. A crowd estimated by the *San Antonio Express* at 1,100 showed up for the game.

McCloskey was nicknamed "Honest John" for his efforts to promote the game, often to his own detriment. That first year he tried to keep the league relatively balanced by moving some of the better players to weaker teams. He sent third baseman James Flynn to San Antonio to help the struggling squad of mostly amateur players that staggered through the first weeks of the season.

But it wasn't enough. The San Antonio team folded on May 24 after a 6–28 start, and Fort Worth quit operations the next month. Even Austin, with the best players in the league, struggled financially, to the point where the team left town for a July Fourth road series and never came back. McCloskey found new backers in San Antonio and transferred his team there to finish the season.

San Antonio did not field a team in 1889, so McCloskey and a core group of his players moved on to Houston, where they won pennants in 1889 and 1892. He ran the club in his hometown of Louisville in 1895–96 and managed Dallas in 1897–98. After that, his career really began to branch out. In 1899, he was an umpire in both the Southern League and the Texas League. Then he went to the West Coast and helped start the predecessor to the Pacific Coast League, serving as a manager.

He got his shot at the big leagues in 1906–08, managing the St. Louis Cardinals, but did not distinguish himself (he had the worst record in major league history for managers involved in at least three hundred games, .312, 197–434). Undaunted, he returned to Texas to start the Rio Grande Valley League in 1914 and managed El Paso in 1915. He even organized military leagues during World War I. In fact, he played a part in the formation of at least ten leagues and managed forty-seven teams in cities from San Francisco to Wilmington, Delaware, from Montgomery, Alabama, to Great Falls, Montana.

In addition, he turned out to have a good eye for talent, scouting and signing a number of big-leaguers, among them Hall of Famers Honus Wagner, Joe Tinker, Jimmy Collins, and Fred Clarke. Even into his seventies, he was working in baseball, helping reorganize the Kitty League in the Midwest in 1932.

He died in November 1940 from the effects of a stroke. His hometown newspaper, the *Louisville Courier-Journal*, paid tribute with a series of photos and a long obituary, which included insight into his life in baseball: "'Honest John' never made any money from any league he organized. To effect the organization of a league, he would take the weakest town in the proposed circuit, a town nobody else wanted. Frequently, the town he took was the one to fold. He often paid players on defunct clubs out of his own pocket. And during the winter he spent his own money turning the ground in virgin baseball territory, for the planting of the seed of professional baseball."

McCloskey died broke and feeling abandoned by the game he had devoted his life to building. In a letter to Texas League president Alvin Gardner in 1938, he said he was owed $4,000 in salary from ball clubs around the country. "But let me owe one dollar, and I am put down as a crook," he noted.

But McCloskey was honored posthumously all over the country. The city of Louisville erected a monument in his honor in the 1940s. He was named to the Texas Sports Hall of Fame in 1962. And perhaps the biggest honor was bestowed by Texan League historian William Ruggles, who simply called McCloskey "the father of the Texas League." "For 70 years, he was still the same John McCloskey Texas knew in 1888—an outdoor man, firm as a lance—young in legs that took him around the base paths in Akron in 1927 in 19 seconds!" Ruggles wrote in *The History of the Texas League* in 1951, "If there was ever a true embodiment of the spirit of baseball, it walked in John McCloskey."

=3=
JESS DERRICK AND LEFTY HAMILTON

FOR DECADES, THE TEXAS LEAGUE RECORD BOOK CREDITED the league's first no-hitter to an obscure Dallas Griffins pitcher named August "Lefty" Hamilton, who blanked the Fort Worth Panthers 3–0 on July 4, 1902. Hamilton played two years in the Texas League and one in the South Texas League and then, apparently, disappeared from the game. There are no records of him having played minor-league baseball anywhere else.

Even in 1902, his one big moment was overshadowed. The Texas League's headline from the same day came out of Corsicana, where the powerful Oil City Oilers won their twenty-sixth game in a row en route to a record twenty-eight straight. They would go on to a league-best 86–22 mark. One hundred years later, our research will cause Hamilton's feat, all but unrecognized at the time, to slip even further into oblivion. It turns out that his was the second nine-inning no-hitter in league history.

On June 24, 1889, Jess Derrick—whose Texas League career lasted just two seasons—threw a no-hitter for Waco against Austin, also by the winning score of 3–0. No one paid any attention to his feat either: the newspapers of the day devoted most of their short game stories to criticizing the umpiring of J.F. Guerher: "[Derrick] put the ball over the plate in great style and rattled the Austin boys so that they could not hit the ball," the *Austin Democratic Statesman* reported. "The Waco club played good ball to a man, and had to contend with the umpire, who seemed to be biased in favor of the visitors."

In any case, Derrick was dominating. He struck out ten and walked three, and just two outfield outs were recorded. He went on to a less than stellar record, though, leading the league in losses in 1889 and earning twenty-four of Waco's thirty-three setbacks. He was out of the league a year later. But he reappeared in the Texas League eighteen years later, working as an umpire in 1908–09. In fact, he was involved in another classic on June 21, 1908. He was the game's lone official when San Antonio's Fred Winchell threw eleven no-hit innings against Waco, then gave up a hit in the twelfth, and took the loss in the thirteenth. There was no criticism of the umpire in the game story from that contest.

=4=
THE 19-RUN INNING

THE 1896 SEASON WAS ONE TO FORGET FOR SAN ANTONIO baseball fans. Their Bronchos were inept almost from opening day. Two managers were fired during the course of the season. The team finished twenty-three games behind the pennant-winning Houston Buffs. Even the newspapers were fed up with the team, to the point of sarcasm. The most telling example came in editions of June 30, on a game that didn't even involve the local team: "The Season's Record," stated the headline on the *San Antonio Express*'s sports page. "Even the Bronchos Never Did Anything Quite So Bad as This." The story referred to a nineteen-run inning given up by the Galveston Sand Crabs in a 31–4 loss to the Fort Worth Panthers.

Galveston, which actually wound up the season in second place, had just rallied from a 6–0 deficit to make it 6–4 going into the bottom of the fourth inning. The Sand Crabs had journeyman pitcher A.C. Burris on the mound. Most of the details of the explosion have, mercifully, been lost to time. But the report in the *Dallas Morning News* noted that the Sand Crabs "vied with each other to see who could do the most booting with the ball, and they 'muffed' flies and made wild throws; in fact, all the miserable playing they could possibly do."

OTHER BIG INNINGS AND BIG GAMES

The history of the Texas League is littered with big comebacks, big innings, and high-scoring games. Some are the result of the conditions—especially the altitude and wind in Midland and El Paso—and some are just the result of bad pitching, back luck, or bad defense.

One of the biggest innings came early in league history. On April 27, 1895, as the league was still struggling to survive, Shreveport scored 14 runs in the fifth inning of a game against Sherman and wound up winning 21–20.

In 1898 Houston Buffs manager George Reed sparked an 11-run fourth-inning rally against San Antonio. The Buffs managed 23 hits—Reed had 5 of them—in coming back from a 4–1 deficit to win 24–11.

In 1925 the Fort Worth Cats scored 10 runs in the fifth inning of a 29–9 pasting of the San Antonio Bears. "It was probably the worst drubbing that was ever administered to a San Antonio team rated as a championship contender," the *San Antonio Express* grumped. The day before, the Cats' Ziggy Sears had driven in 11 runs in Fort Worth's 19–8 romp over the Bears. The next day, Fort Worth won 24–12, topping off the series. In that game, San Antonio pitcher Bob Couchman and a policeman named O'Banion served as umpires after the original pair left the game under police protection following particularly threatening language from the home fans. The veteran

Fort Worth had 12 hits—8 singles, 2 doubles, a triple, and a home run—in the inning, and the Sand Crabs were charged with 4 errors and a passed ball. The Panthers sent twenty-four men to the plate. Of the 31 runs Fort Worth scored that day—on 28 hits—the official box score listed just 5 as being earned. Galveston was charged with 10 errors, including 2 each by left fielder J.G. Brott, first baseman William "Farmer" Works and Burris, who moved to second base when George "Piggy" Page came on in relief during the disastrous inning. Will McDevitt, who was listed as one of two amateurs in the Fort Worth lineup, did the most damage on the day. Hitting ninth, he went 5 for 6 with a triple.

THE TEXAS LEAGUE'S GREATEST HITS = 21

Couchman, who was not playing that day, was a compromise choice of both managers.

On May 5, 1983, with wind gusts of up to thirty-five miles per hour blowing toward the fences of Midland's Christensen Stadium, the hometown Cubs scored 11 runs in the bottom of the first against the El Paso Diablos. Fifteen batters came to the plate, with 3 of them getting 2 hits each. In the top of the second, the Diablos sent 17 men to the plate—13 of them got hits—and went ahead 13–11. Midland answered with 5 more in the bottom of the inning. El Paso scored 4 more in the third. It was 17–16 after three innings. Fortunately, some semblance of pitching returned, and the winds died down a little. El Paso won, 20–19, with a run in the top of the ninth.

On June 15, 1998, Arkansas rallied from deficits of 4–0, 9–4, and 20–13 to beat Jackson 21–20 on a home run by Tyrone Horne in the bottom of the tenth. The teams combined for 49 hits, 20 of them for extra bases. "I've never seen anything like that in my life," Arkansas manager Chris Maloney told *Baseball America*.

Later that summer, the Wichita Wranglers went to the eleventh inning in a scoreless tie with the San Antonio Missions, and the Wranglers had the usually dependable Steve Prihoda on the mound. Before the top of the inning was over, the Missions had scored twelve runs on ten hits, including a grand slam and a solo home run by San Antonio catcher Angel Pena, who went 5 for 5 on the night. ★

The *Galveston Daily News* was not amused with the results, if its headlines were any indication:

GETS MONOTONOUS

Sand Crabs Are Again Trampled

Under Foot by the

Panthers

THEY WEREN'T IN IT AT ALL

In the *San Antonio Express*, the sneering headline read "The Panthers Made Monkeys of the Sand Crabs."

Only one other team has ever come close to the record—the

1930 Waco Cubs, who scored 18 runs in an inning against Beaumont. The next-biggest inning was 14 runs, accomplished most recently by Shreveport in a 19–2 victory over Tulsa on May 22, 2002.

=5=
BILL KEMMER

ALTHOUGH HE HAD BEEN TO THE MAJOR LEAGUES, HAVING played in eleven games for the National League's Louisville Colonels in 1895, Bill Kemmer didn't stick there. And once he got to Texas later that year, he moved around a lot, playing for six teams in seven years. But the 6-foot-2, 195-pound native of Pennsylvania made himself a place in the league's record book early in the 1898 season while playing for the Houston Buffs.

The Fort Worth Panthers were in Houston on April 18, 1898, and the game almost had to be called off because of rain (newspaper reports from the next day said "the grounds were muddy and the fielders were thereby handicapped.") The hitters, on the other hand, were not slowed down at all, as the Buffs pounded 18 hits and the Panthers 12 in Houston's 16–10 victory. But the most remarkable hitting statistics belonged to Bill Kemmer.

In six at-bats, the twenty-one-year-old first baseman had 5 hits—three 3-run home runs and a pair of singles that produced 3 additional runs. In all, he drove in 12 runs, second only to the 16 by Jay Clarke in Corsicana's 51–3 victory over Texarkana in 1902.

"The whole baseball part of the town is talking about it tonight," the *Houston Post* reported the next day. "Kemmer is really worthy of all the praise that can be said of him—six times up, three home runs, two singles, and he hit the ball hard every time."

"To put it in a nutshell, Kemmer won the game for Houston." His final homer came in the bottom of the ninth, "and the crowd went wild," the *San Antonio Express* reported.

Kemmer—who was born William Edward Kemmerer on November 15, 1873—had shown his hitting prowess before. In the last forty-three games of the 1895 season, he had hit .405 for Shreveport. The records are sketchy for the final seasons of the nineteenth century, but it's clear that Kemmer topped .300 each year—in 1896 and 1899 for Galveston and in 1897 for Denison-Sherman and Waco. In 1898, the record is clearer—he hit .366 in thirty-four games for the Buffs in the abbreviated season that ended May 13 because of the Spanish-American War.

Kemmer went missing after that, but he showed up again in Texas in 1905, when he was one of eight men who managed the hapless Galveston Sand Crabs of the South Texas League. The next season, he was the manager of the dreadful Lake Charles club in the same league, a team that went 30–94 and finished last in the six-team circuit.

=6=
CORSICANA 51, TEXARKANA 3

J. DOAK ROBERTS HAD IT ALL FIGURED OUT IN THE SPRING OF 1902. Roberts had landed a team in the newly reconstituted Texas League team for the east Texas oil boomtown of Corsicana. Armed with an oil-boom budget, he had gone out and signed up a top-notch collection of players.

The Oil City Oilers were managed by Big Mike O'Connor, who had been around the league since its beginnings. He had played for or managed teams in Fort Worth, Austin, San Antonio, Sherman, Dallas, and Denison between 1888 and 1901, some of them more than once. Corsicana's first professional baseball team also featured infielders J. Walter Morris and Hunter Hill, both future big-leaguers, and William "Lucky" Wright, the league's top pitcher, who also made it to the big leagues and later served as a Texas League umpire. The Oilers had some veterans from earlier days of the Texas League, including Ike Pendleton, who would play ten seasons in the league, and third baseman George Markley, who would play on four championship teams in eight years in the circuit.

Roberts's team was by far the best in the state, jumping to the top of the standings from the first week of the season. Fans flocked to Oil City Park on the town's south side to see the team whip up on the rest of the league, which was far less successful (the

Sherman-Denison entry lost its first ten games and bolted for Texarkana, and only one other team, Dallas, came close to playing better than .500 ball).

But Roberts hadn't planned for everything. Corsicana had strictly enforced blue laws, which forbade most kinds of business on Sundays—including professional sports. For some reason the Oil City Oilers scheduled a game against Texarkana on Sunday, June 15.

Most baseball teams in the early part of the twentieth century weren't big moneymakers, so it was important to play a game on the day that would guarantee a big crowd. Roberts checked around and found that Ennis, a town thirty-five miles to the north, had a ballpark and no blue laws. The ballpark wasn't big—the right-field foul pole was reported in various places to be anywhere from 140 to 210 feet from home plate, and the rest of the dimensions were almost as cozy—but it was a place to play.

Roberts convinced Texarkana's management—which would get a share of the gate—to agree to move the game. That was Texarkana's first mistake. The second was sending a pitcher named DeWitt to the mound. The historical records are fuzzy on his identity. There was a DeWitt listed as a part-owner of the team, and some reports said he was the pitcher that day. Other reports said the pitcher was DeWitt's son, whom the team's manager had been forced to use.

In any case, he was on the mound for what turned out to be the biggest whipping in league history, and perhaps in all of professional baseball. In a reported two hours and ten minutes, the Oilers scored 51 runs on 59 hits, including 20 home runs. Texarkana scored 3 runs and did not hit a ball out of the park.

The star that day was a nineteen-year-old Canadian named Jay Justin Clarke, nicknamed "Nig" because of his dark Indian complexion (these were not exactly politically correct times, after all). Clarke was the Oilers' catcher, a left-handed hitter whose biggest accomplishment up to that point had been working with the best pitchers in the league.

Clarke hit a home run his first time up. And the next. And the next after that. Before the day was done, in fact, Clarke had hit 8 home runs in 8 at-bats and driven in anywhere from 16 to 20 runs (the run batted in, or RBI, was not an official statistic at the time, and as one newspaper report said, the official scorekeeper might have been more than a little overwhelmed).

At one point, a wealthy cattleman came out of the stands and pressed a $50 bill into Clarke's hand. The next time Clarke hit one out, another cattleman ("the rival cattle baron," Clarke said in an interview much later) came out and matched it. A hat passed through the stands for the star of the game wound up with $185 in it, far more than a month's salary. As soon as he had a chance, Clarke did the logical thing with the cash—he spent it on hats and clothes, a decade's worth.

Skepticism about the day's enormous statistics began almost immediately. One newspaper report said, "Mike O'Connor is enterprising all right. The official scorer lost his head but the foxy manager of the Oil City boys has discovered a tabulated record which goes as the official figures. He realizes the benefits in swelling batting averages."

There were other doubters as well. In one wire service report, Clarke's homer total was changed from eight to three because either an editor or a teletype operator assumed the total was a typographic error. The fact that none of the box scores from the game actually added up contributed to the debate, both then and in the intervening hundred-plus years. Baseball statisticians through the years have tried to prove that there was no way Clarke could have hit eight home runs on that sunny Sunday in Ennis.

But Texas League historian William Ruggles believed in Clarke's achievement. In 1916, he got sworn reports from the scorekeeper at Ennis as well as from Roberts and Morris, who

MOST RBIs IN A TEXAS LEAGUE GAME

16	June 15, 1902	Jay "Nig" Clarke	Corsicana
12	April 18, 1898	Bill Kemmer	Fort Worth
11	May 19, 1925	John "Ziggy" Sears	Fort Worth
10	April 24, 1954	Bill Gabler	Fort Worth
10	June 8, 1959	Frank Howard	Victoria
10	July 27, 1998	Tyrone Horne	Arkansas
9	June 27, 1936	Sig Gryska	San Antonio
9	June 16, 1948	Charlie Grant	San Antonio
9	September 1, 1950	Wally Post	Tulsa
9	May 29, 1961	Al Nagel	Amarillo
9	June 9, 1963	Ron Campbell	Amarillo
9	July 25, 1967	Tom Egan	El Paso
9	May 30, 1972	Terry McDermott	El Paso
9	May 10, 1973	Bob Frazier	Amarillo
9	June 18, 1980	Tom Brunansky	El Paso
9	May 5, 1981	John Alvarez	Amarillo
9	April 30, 1983	Mike Felder	El Paso
9	August 10, 1998	Todd Dunn	El Paso
9	April 8, 2000	Craig Monroe	Tulsa

both went on to serve as president of the league. And in an interview in 1947, Clarke was sure he had hit the eight homers. It was, after all, the highlight of his professional career, which lasted twenty-five years and included parts of nine undistinguished seasons in the majors.

The game still has a big place in the Texas League record book, marks that will never be matched: Clarke's eight home runs, and the most runs, hits, home runs, total bases, and at-bats in a game.

The scheduling mistake was about the only error Roberts made that season. The 51–3 game was number nine in a league-record twenty-eight-game winning streak, and Corsicana finished the year 86–22, a .796 winning percentage that has never been matched. The Oilers finished 28½ games ahead of second-place Dallas, a margin topped only once.

=7=
SIS BATEMAN

MANY OF THE EARLY STARS OF THE TEXAS LEAGUE ARE remembered for their feats (like the eight home runs hit by Jay Clarke in a game for Corsicana) or their longevity (like the 1,777 league contests played in by Paul Easterling). But others have all but been lost in the fog of time. Such is the case of Henry Quaite Bateman, who was known as both "Clyde" and "Sis" Bateman in the Texas League.

Bateman was born on Christmas Day, 1875, in Melissa, a small town northeast of Dallas. His father, Patrick Henry Bateman, had served in the Confederate army during the Civil War and survived the battle of Gettysburg. At some point after the war, he moved to Texas and became a teacher. Little else is known about the family or about Sis Bateman's early years. In fact, he already was twenty-six years old when he played his first recorded professional game, pitching for Fort Worth in 1902. In that complete-game victory, he allowed 1 run and 4 hits, walked 2, and struck out 12. He also went 4 for 5 at the plate.

Resurrected in 1902 after a two-year hiatus, the Texas League had four teams for the 1903 season—Dallas, Fort Worth, Corsicana, and a fourth franchise, owned by Ted Sullivan, which didn't have a home until Sullivan settled on Paris in March.

Although referred to by other names, the team was commonly known as the Parisians. Sullivan, who also was the field manager, signed a handful of notable players in an attempt to bring a winner to northeast Texas. One was pitcher Cy Mulkey, who was a lawyer and the brother of noted Texas evangelist Abe Mulkey. Cy had broken into the league in 1895 and eventually would play for eleven clubs in twelve Texas League cities as well as manage and serve as an umpire. Sullivan also signed infielder Mickey Coyle, who was in the second of his seven seasons in the league. Catcher Roland Wolfe was one of three players on the roster who had spent part of the 1902 season in Fort Worth, along with pitcher Reeves McKay and Sis Bateman.

Bateman's ability to both pitch effectively and hit showed up right away, as Paris got off to a fast start. By May 14, the Parisians were already running away from the four-team league, at 12–5; Corsicana and Fort Worth were 8–10, and Dallas was 7–10.

Corsicana's Oil City Oilers were not the same club as in 1902, when they had dominated the league, and by 1903 the club's small park had become a favorite spot for opposing hitters. On the afternoon of May 14, the Parisians feasted on Lucky Wright, one of Corsicana's aces from the year before. Paris had 24 hits—9 of them home runs—and won, 13–7. Wolfe hit 3 home runs, an outstanding day for any player. But he was overshadowed by Bateman, who hit 4 out of the park and added a triple for a 5-for-5 day.

The Parisians finished the first half far in front, with a record of 32–20. But attendance in Paris disappointed Sullivan, who did not have the deepest pockets in the league. When the second half started, the team moved to Waco and was renamed the Steers, but not all the players made the move, and the team struggled.

Sis Bateman stuck with the club, though, making regular starts on the mound and playing in the outfield. On July 11, he matched his four-homer day with a historic performance on the mound.

For five innings, he did not allow a Fort Worth batter to reach base. In the sixth, he walked a Panther—and then got a double-play ball. In the ninth, he walked his mound opponent, Harry Lockhead, but stranded him at first to end the game. It was the fourth nine-inning no-hitter in the history of the league, and the first—and only one—by a player who had hit four home runs in a game.

Bateman went on to hit .344 in eighty-eight games, with a league-high 9 triples. He tied Wolfe for the league lead in home runs, with 13. As a pitcher, he was 18–15 with 119 strikeouts and 32 complete games in 35 starts. The Paris-Waco club struggled down the stretch and lost to Dallas, 7 games to 3, in the postseason.

The next year, Bateman played for Milwaukee in the American Association, but he had just six decisions as a pitcher and hit .287. In seven more seasons, he never matched what he had done in the Texas League, topping .300 just once more. His last year as a player was 1910, when he played seventy-three games for Monmouth-Burlington in the Central Association. He died on January 18, 1937, in Milwaukee, where he had played for parts of five seasons.

=8=
JACK HUFFMEISTER

ON MOST DAYS, GIVING UP ONE HIT AND WALKING ONE BATTER in eleven innings would be good enough to earn a pitcher a victory, but July 14, 1904, was not one of those days.

Jack Huffmeister was the starter for the Dallas Giants that Thursday afternoon, taking on the Fort Worth Panthers. He was all but unhittable, allowing just a single to Panthers right fielder Dee Poindexter. But the Panthers scored 6 runs—all unearned—against him as the Giants committed an astounding 16 errors. The Panthers pitcher, Harold Christman, a Texas League veteran who went on to win 21 games that year, allowed 13 hits and walked 2. He gave up 5 runs in pitching an 11-inning complete game for the 6–5 win.

It was all those errors: 4 by shortstop Aaron Mott, 3 each by first baseman Fred Hunter and second baseman George Andres, and 2 each by third baseman Ota Johnson, right fielder W.L. Miller, and Huffmeister. "Terrible throws, fancy fumbles and bum bungles gave the visitors many a life on first base, and when they [didn't] get there it had to be a strike out or a fly to Doyle or Ury," the *Dallas Morning News* reported, referring to left fielder Billy Doyle and center fielder Lon Ury, neither of whom had an error for Dallas. "After making thirteen safe hits as against the lonely single for Fort Worth, they presented the baseball world with the remarkable spectacle of sixteen errors and inglorious defeat for themselves," the *San Antonio Daily Express* reported.

The only other player in the Giants' lineup not charged with an error was the catcher, Branch Rickey. In the first of two seasons with Dallas, Rickey was on his way to a brief major-league playing career—and a Hall of Fame career as an innovator in the front offices of the St. Louis Cardinals, Brooklyn Dodgers, and Pittsburgh Pirates. On July 14, 1904, Rickey did a solid job behind the plate, as Fort Worth runners did not steal a base.

The sixteen errors in a game tied a league record set in 1895, and it remains a league record today. Huffmeister appeared in eleven games for the Giants in 1904 and never played in the Texas League again.

=9=
HICKORY DICKSON
AND RICK ADAMS

IN THE HISTORY OF THE TEXAS LEAGUE, FORTY CITIES AND
towns, from Jackson, Mississippi, to El Paso have fielded teams.
Few, though, can match the success of the Cleburne Railroaders in
a single season. In its only season in the league, 1906, Cleburne
won a pennant, produced two no-hitters, played in the longest
scoreless game in league history, and fielded a player who would
later become a member of the Baseball Hall of Fame. The
Railroaders also benefited from one of the league's greatest pitching performances to clinch the championship.

It all began with a meeting of the North Texas League's owners, who were trying to merge—without success—with the six-
team South Texas League to form a statewide organization.
Failing that, they at least wanted more than four teams, since
interest and attendance had dwindled in 1905 as the same squads
kept playing each other again and again.

League president J. Doak Roberts and the league's strongest
owners—those in Dallas, Fort Worth, and Waco—decided to add
teams in Cleburne and Greenville. Roberts had operated the
Temple Boll Weevils in 1905, with Prince Ben Shelton as manager, but in 1906 Shelton was named the manager in Cleburne.
He recruited the two best pitchers from the Boll Weevils, Rick

Adams and Walter "Hickory" Dickson, as well as catcher William Powell, second baseman Mickey Coyle, third baseman Roy Akin, outfielder Dee Poindexter, utility infielder Zena Clayton, and pitcher-outfielder Cal Lewis. Early in the season, Cleburne also traded for another strong player, center fielder George Whiteman, who was in the early stages of a career that would include eleven seasons in the Texas League and a starring role for the Boston Red Sox in the 1918 World Series, the Sox' last World Series title until 2004.

Shelton and team president Phil Allen also signed a couple of strong rookies: twenty-one-year-old Dode Criss, a hard-throwing pitcher and harder-hitting batter, and Tris Speaker, an eighteen-year-old pitcher from Hubbard. Criss would go on to hit .396 that year, but he did not have enough at-bats to claim the batting title. Speaker, a right-hander, was a washout on the mound—he lost his first seven starts—but his blazing speed made him an asset in the outfield and on the bases, where he stole thirty-three bases in eighty-four games and hit .268, third highest on the team. Speaker would go on to lead the league in hitting in 1907 and to play twenty-two years in the majors and manage the Cleveland Indians. He was among the original five players voted into the Baseball Hall of Fame.

But Cleburne's strength in 1906 wasn't at the plate or on the bases—it was in the arms of pitchers Adams and Dickson.

On June 3, the Railroaders were scheduled to play a double-header at Waco. The first game, with Adams on the mound, remained scoreless through nine innings and went into extra innings. Finally, Cleburne broke through in the fourteenth to score five times. Adams, who threw all fourteen innings for the Railroaders, retired the Waco Navigators without incident in the bottom of the inning to finish off a 2-hitter. He also struck out 15 and walked just 1.

Dickson matched him at the end of June, throwing a no-hitter against Temple. The Boll Weevils managed to score an unearned run in the top of the first but did not have another serious threat in the 5–1 victory for the Railroaders (in the second game of the doubleheader that day, Speaker won to snap his losing streak as a pitcher).

On July 23, Dickson started a game against first-half champ Fort Worth and the Panthers' ace, Alex Dupree. Neither pitcher allowed a run through the first nine innings, and the game went into extra innings. Whiteman, Cleburne's center fielder, threw out Dupree at the plate, and a Fort Worth runner was also thrown out trying to score from second on an error by Dickson. As the game wore on, the *Fort Worth Telegram* reported that "the players were so tired they could scarcely drag themselves to their positions; the setting sun cast the shadow of the grandstand far out across the infield and halfway over the outfield; the pitchers' arms moved more like machines than flesh and blood, but still the two teams struggled for the lead that never came." The game lasted for more than two hours (a long time in the days before commercial breaks and between-innings promotions) and nineteen innings, as the teams played until the game was called because of darkness. It is still the longest scoreless game in league history.

Adams matched Dickson's no-hitter on August 23, shutting down Waco 6–0 in the second game of a doubleheader, as Cleburne kept pace with Fort Worth and Dallas for the second-half title. Adams held off the Panthers 6–5 on September 1, leaving just a doubleheader between the teams on September 2 to decide the winner.

Dickson started the first game and beat the Panthers 2–0 on a six-hitter, with Speaker, Poindexter, and Whiteman running down long fly balls in the outfield to preserve the shutout. And then, with Adams worn out from the day before and Shelton saving Criss for a makeup game the next day, Dickson started the second game. The result was the same, a 2–0 six-hitter, clinching the second-half title for the Railroaders. "It was the greatest feat of (Dickson's) life," the *Cleburne Morning Review* reported. "The mighty batters of the Panthers were cut down or caught out, and notwithstanding the fact that they smashed the air, clouted the ball from fence to fence and high in the air, the nimble fingers of some one of the Railroaders were always there to take in the horsehide, as accepting a gift from some friend."

The next day's game was rained out, and then Fort Worth— which had lost six of its last seven games with Cleburne—refused to take part in the scheduled playoff between first-half and second-half winners for some unknown reason. The Railroaders were declared the league's champions.

Adams finished the year 25–13 and led the league in appearances (40) and strikeouts (138); he took off for St. Paul of the American Association immediately after the Texas League pennant was decided.

Dickson, who had been nicknamed "Hickory" by the local fans because he had recovered from a shoulder injury as though his bones were made from the tough wood, finished with a record of 24–12. He went on to pitch in the National League and the Federal League, compiling losing records for the Boston Braves in 1912 and 1913 and for the Federal League's Pittsburgh Rebels in 1914. The next season, he went 7–5 for the Rebels at the age of thirty-six. He died just three years later of pneumonia in Ardmore, Oklahoma.

=10=
AUSTIN 44,
SAN ANTONIO 0

THE PHRASE *UMPIRE BAITING* **WASN'T AROUND IN 1907, BUT** for the San Antonio Bronchos, it wasn't because they weren't trying. That season, the Bronchos were well-known around the Texas League for riding the umpires, protesting virtually every close call. What was worse—at least for the league's umpires—was that the club was good. They had a solid lineup of veterans, including two players who would go on to manage San Antonio, and two of the best pitchers in the league, twenty-three-game-winner Buck Harris and twenty-two-game-winner E. M. Colgrove.

San Antonio was in a three-way race for the league lead with Austin and Dallas on July 23 when the Bronchos went to Austin's Riverside Park for a doubleheader with the Senators. The Bronchos were leading 5–4 in the bottom of the eighth of the first contest when the Senators' Eddie Cermack slid past third base and was tagged by the third baseman Frank Everhardt. But umpire Jack Schuster—who in the common practice of the time was the only umpire on the field—called him safe. The Bronchos players lit into him in singles and pairs, then cleared out to let Manager Sam LaRocque, who was playing center field, have his say. After blistering Schuster, LaRocque was ejected. First baseman Pat Newnam then argued with Schuster, and he too was tossed from the game, escorted away by an Austin policeman. At that point, the Bronchos walked off the field, and Schuster declared the game a forfeit win for the Senators.

San Antonio's players were ready to go home at that point, but someone realized that with the second game of a doubleheader left to be played, there would be a substantial fine for the team if they left—a fine that might come out of their salaries. So they decided to play. At least they appeared to play.

Infielder Art Griggs was the starting pitcher in the second game. He gave up twelve runs in the first inning, as the Bronchos let routine ground balls roll through their legs and lazy pop-ups fall untouched. Another infielder, Ike Pendleton, came on to relieve Griggs and was no more successful. George "Cap" Leidy, a former minor-league manager who would inherit the manager's job the next season, also made his only career pitching appearance. Players in the field went from one position to another, turning the game into a scorekeeper's nightmare (it would be almost twenty years before players wore numbers, and the exasperated reporters noted that "it is impossible to give a correct box score of this game").

Recognizing an opportunity to pad their statistics, the Senators racked up 35 hits and 23 stolen bases. The final score was 44 – 0, the most lopsided shutout in league history. Most of the fans were amused at the spectacle, which the *San Antonio Express* said resembled "all the comedy acts known to the circus ring." "Home runs were common and such ridiculous plays were made that the game was enjoyable," the paper's Austin bureau reported.

Some weren't so pleased. A petition was circulated in Austin and sent to league president William Robbie, complaining about the Bronchos' conduct. "Such work will not be offered the people of this city again," the *Austin Democratic Statesman* said in its game story.

If there were any ramifications for the Bronchos, they weren't reported in print. However, LaRocque suddenly resigned his position on July 29, less than a week after the game, to take care of some unspecified personal business in Canada. Austin and San Antonio continued to battle for the pennant, with the race going down to the final weeks of the season. The Senators finally pulled away, winning the pennant by 3½ games.

=11=
HARRY ABLES

IN MORE THAN 110 SEASONS OF TEXAS LEAGUE BASEBALL, thousands of pitchers have come through the league. Some, like Dizzy Dean and Dennis Eckersley, were bound for the Baseball Hall of Fame. Others, like Bob Turley and Eric Gagne, went on to win the Cy Young award. A few played in the World Series and the Major League All-Star game.

But none of them have been able to match four records set by Harry Ables in 1910. That season, the long-armed left-hander from Terrell, Texas, struck out an amazing 310 hitters, a mark that has been seriously challenged only once—by Dean, who fanned 303 in 1931. Ables also set a record for consecutive strikeouts, getting 10 to start a game against Dallas on August 6, 1910. And in a game on July 5 of that year, he pitched twenty-three innings— the final twenty-two of them without allowing a run. Both are still league records as well.

It was that kind of year for the 6-foot-4, twenty-five-year old pitcher.

The San Antonio Bronchos knew what they were getting when they acquired Ables from Dallas during the 1908 season. In 1905, he was the first pitcher in league history to win both ends of a doubleheader, throwing back-to-back shutouts against Fort Worth. In 1907, he was 12–5 and struck out 126 in 158 innings.

The acquisition of the left-hander—who could hide a ball in his huge hands—helped spur the Bronchos to the pennant in 1908, as he wound up a combined 15–6 with 142 strikeouts in twenty-four games. In 1909, he pitched well enough to earn a five-game trial with the American League's Cleveland Naps, but he returned to San Antonio the next spring.

Ables's amazing 1910 season got off to a great start. He struck out the first 7 batters against Oklahoma City on April 27 and wound up with a 4-hit, 15-strikeout performance, as San Antonio won, 1–0. "On the pinions of some of the greatest baseball ever pitched by Harry Ables—and that is praise enough for any sucker—the locals swept to an even break with the Indians yesterday afternoon," the *San Antonio Daily Express* reported. "The big boy liked the warm afternoon, and from start to finish he had all his stuff." "He had a drop ball working that almost broke the batter's back when he attempted to connect with it, and twirled in mid-season form," the *San Antonio Light* reported.

On June 13, Ables held the Dallas Giants hitless through 10⅔ innings before shortstop Jewel Ens singled. But the Giants did not take advantage of the hit, or of a single and two stolen bases by Tony Thebo in the fourteenth. In the bottom of the inning, Otto McIver walked, bringing up George Stinson. On a hit-and-run play, Stinson fouled off the pitch from Dallas's Liz Torrey. Then, trying to sacrifice, Stinson bunted foul. Finally, on a 3–2 pitch, Stinson swung away—and hit the ball onto Flores Street, outside the left-field fence. In the scoring of the day, only McIver—who did a backflip as he crossed home plate—scored on the home run, giving Ables a 1–0 victory. He struck out nineteen and allowed just four base runners in fourteen innings. "[Ables] sported a curve that started at the shoulder and sluffed off until it struck the ground," the *San Antonio Light* reported. "Four Giants swung at third strikes that hit in front of the plate." Still, San Antonio fans had been nervous the whole afternoon and were relieved only when Stinson finally delivered a big hit. "Fans had seen Ables pitch so many wonderful games, only to lose by a fluke, that they were scared blind half the time," the *Light* noted.

On July 5, Ables and Waco's Arthur Loudell hooked up in a battle for the ages. The Navigators scored a run off Ables in the top of the first and then were shut out for twenty-two innings. San Antonio tied it in the sixth but could not scratch out another run against Loudell. "It was the crowning work of Ables," the *Light* reported. "That is, it set to rest all gossips as to his ability to go the long route, for there never was a time when he faltered. He showed the same high-class article of ball in the twenty-third session as he showed in the early stages of the game." Only San Antonio's anemic offense kept him from getting a victory. The Bronchos, who eventually finished third in the league, left 16 runners on base. Ables recorded 17 strikeouts and allowed 16 hits in the four-hour, fifteen-minute game, which was called because of darkness and which forced the postponement of the second game of a doubleheader scheduled for that day.

On August 8, against the best team in the league, the Dallas Giants, Ables was masterful again. He struck out the first ten Dallas hitters he faced that afternoon, a group that included Hank Gowdy, who would go on to win the batting title, and Harry Storch, who tied with Gowdy for the league's home-run lead. Ables wound up with fifteen strikeouts and a 4–2 victory. "They were lucky to get a foul off his delivery at any time and four hits were the limit of the Giants," the *Express* reported. "Ables never appeared in better form. He appeared to roll the ball in his hand like a marble and absolutely flip them at the plate."

And then in his final start for the Bronchos, Ables was part of a tandem that turned in one of the most dominant days of pitching in league history. In the first game of a doubleheader against Waco, he pitched a seven-inning no-hitter and won 1–0. In the second game, teammate Fred Blanding allowed one hit and also won 1–0. (Teams had the option of playing seven- or nine-inning games in doubleheaders of the time.)" One dispectic [*sic*] hit—an

MOST STRIKEOUTS IN A TEXAS LEAGUE GAME

22	August 11, 1951	Bob Turley	San Antonio	(16 innings, No Decision)
21	July 16, 1978	Dave Righetti	Tulsa	(9 innings, No Decision)
20	August 21, 1909	Willie Mitchell	San Antonio	(W)
19	June 13, 1910	Harry Ables	San Antonio	(14 innings, W)
19	May 21, 1946	John Van Cuyk	Fort Worth	(W)
19	June 6, 1972	Dennis James	El Paso	(W)
18	July 30, 1930	Lil Stoner	Fort Worth	(W)
18	August 15, 1951	Wilmer Mizell	Houston (W)	
18	June 28, 1955	Ryne Duren	San Antonio	(W)
18	August 14, 1955	Don Ferrarese	San Antonio	(W)
18	June 21, 1961	Danilo Rivas	Victoria	(10 innings, L)
18	August 15, 1961	Danilo Rivas	Victoria	(9 innings in relief, L)

infield poke that was beaten out in a hot sprint—was the total of Waco's hickory smiting yesterday afternoon in a double-header of seven-inning games," the *Express* reported.

Ables finished the season 19–12. It wasn't even the best record on the team, as Blanding was 20–9. But he had his records.

The left-hander went on to pitch briefly for the New York Yankees in 1911 but was 0–1 in three appearances and finished the season with Oakland in the Pacific Coast League. He led that league in victories (25), strikeouts (303), and walks (134) in 1912 but never again made it to the majors.

He led a group that bought the San Antonio Bears in 1925, and he was president of the club from 1925 to 1928. As a publicity stunt, he pitched in a game for the Bears in 1925 at the age of forty, giving up five hits and three runs in five innings and taking the loss. He did it again in 1926, but that time he got a win with four innings of one-hit ball.

=12=
THE 49-MINUTE GAME

A THUNDERSHOWER LOOMED NEAR GALVESTON'S BEACH
Park on the afternoon of September 7, 1913, the last day of the
Texas League season. The Galveston club management wanted
the day's game between the Pirates and the San Antonio Bronchos
to be played, though, so it wouldn't have to issue rain checks—
rain checks that would have to carry over to the 1914 season.

Both teams had been eliminated from the pennant race weeks
before; San Antonio was on its way to a fourth-place finish and
Galveston was solidly seventh in the eight-team league. The players, weary from a long summer, no doubt were anxious to end the
season. So when the management went to both teams and, as the
Galveston Daily News put it, suggested "a little fast playing would
not be considered amiss," the players were more than happy to
oblige.

The game started early, at 3:55 P.M. The first four innings were
played, as the *Daily News* reported, in "almost the same number of
minutes." The squall line went around the park, but the players
kept up the frantic pace. Galveston scored a single run off San
Antonio starter Brown Rogers in the fourth, and the Pirates' Babe
Hughes hit a solo homer in the fifth—sprinting around the bases,
no doubt. Galveston added a run in the seventh on three infield

OTHER FAST GAMES

The Texas League has had a handful of speedy games to rival the forty-nine-minute Galveston-San Antonio game of 1913.

In 1907, Austin and Houston played nine innings in fifty-seven minutes, with the Buffs winning 1–0. Houston had just two hits and Austin three, and as the *Houston Post* reported, the game was not slowed down by any of the "tiresome spitball foolishness by either hurler." Houston's Elmer Coyle scored the game's only run, in the fourth inning. The final out of the game landed in the glove of the Buffs' right fielder, Tris Speaker, who would start his twenty-two-season big-league career later that year.

Another fast game came in the fading days of the season before the league's World War II hiatus. On August 20, 1942, the San Antonio Missions beat the Dallas Rebels 2–1 in sixty-seven minutes. The two pitchers—Al LaMacchia for the Missions and Hank Perry for the Rebels—were fast workers. LaMacchia didn't like his infielders to throw the ball around after outs, and he had a system with his catcher: he would throw only a fastball or a straight changeup if he didn't get a sign. He often didn't wait for one and threw entire games that way. "I was just a fast worker," LaMacchia said. "Today you sit through games that are 3½ hours long. I could have pitched two games in that time. I can remember walking into the clubhouse the day I was pitching a game and hearing the infielders talking about who was pitching that night. They'd say LaMacchia, and then they'd say 'We're getting out of here fast tonight.' Looking back on it now, I consider that a hell of a compliment." ★

hits and a sacrifice fly and another in the eighth when Red Massey was hit by a pitch with the bases loaded. Those four rallies hardly slowed the pace, though.

"The coolness of the afternoon and the knowledge that the season was over at last seemed to lend unwonted spryness to the athletes and they covered the field like a squad of frolicking jackrabbits, taking all kinds of chances and getting away with them," the *Daily News* reported. When Pirates pitcher C. H. Harben recorded the final out—to earn his twentieth victory of the season—it was 4:44 P.M. The teams had played nine innings in forty-nine minutes, a league record that has never been matched.

Among the amazing facts about the game: Galveston had 13 hits and San Antonio 7, and the Pirates left 9 men on base. But one statistic tells the real story: Harben, who tied for the league strikeout lead with 204, struck out just one man, and Rogers struck out only two. Virtually every hitter swung at the first pitch, and there were no walks issued.

=13=
THE 1914 SEASON

IN MORE THAN A HUNDRED SEASONS OF BASEBALL, THE Texas League has had great teams and awful teams, exciting pennant races and runaways, great rivalries and lopsided matchups. But for a wild ride, it's never had anything to match 1914. Two teams lost more than one hundred games, and one of them was the acknowledged worst team in league history. Four different pitchers threw no-hitters. A runner stole six bases in a game. And the pennant race wasn't decided until November 1, well after the close of the season—and then it was called a tie.

A couple of trends emerged early in the season, when Hatton "Professor" Ogle of Waco threw a no-hitter against Austin on April 26. First, it became clear that the Austin Senators were not very good, and they weren't going to get any better. Second, Waco was good, probably good enough to challenge Houston, which had won Texas League pennants in 1912 and 1913.

The Buffs also established a trend early in the season when they stole 13 bases May 4 against Dallas. "The poor old aged and decrepit Texas League champs crept around the bases yesterday and ran up a league record for the season by making 15 runs and stealing 13 bases," the *Houston Post* reported. "In the face of significant criticism that the team had lost much of its speed on the paths and had deteriorated in hitting since 1913, the showing partakes slightly of the sensational." Houston would go on to steal 14 in a game June 29 against the Austin Senators and 15 against the hapless Senators on July 26, including a league-record 6 by the Buffs' John Frierson in the second game.

The Buffs' success against the Senators wasn't limited to the base paths, though. Houston swept the season series with Austin, all nineteen games. It was one of several dubious marks set by the Senators, who wound up using a record seventy-two players during the season. Austin also set records for most losses (114), longest losing streak (32 games), most errors (424), and lowest winning percentage (.214, going 31–114).

The Senators were owned by Walter Quebedeaux, who started selling off or trading his best players after the team got off to a slow start. He was summoned to a meeting of the league's presidents in Houston, and he assured them that he was working to strengthen his club. But he also pointed out that as long as he was paying the players on the roster and meeting his obligations to the league, they didn't have any cause to interfere with his business.

Quebedeaux never did strengthen the club, and it staggered through June and into the thirty-two-game losing streak. Manager Walter Frantz, no doubt to his relief, was fired midway through the debacle. Charlie Moran finished up the season as manager, ending up with a record of 11–61. Not surprisingly, Quebedeaux sold the team after the season to a group that moved it to Shreveport. He then started over in the Central Texas League, and he also ran that franchise into the ground as the league imploded midway through the 1915 season.

While Austin was setting new records in futility, San Antonio wasn't doing much better. The inept Bronchos, just two years removed from a strong second-place finish, ran through three managers and wound up 46–103.

Meanwhile, Waco and Houston caught and passed Beaumont

at midseason and ran away from the rest of the league. The up-and-coming Waco Navigators had the league's best hitter, Bob Clemens, who wound up leading in batting average (.327), total hits (196), singles (157), runs (115), and total bases (264). Teammate Archie Tanner tied for the league lead in doubles with 34, and Waco pitcher Eddie Donalds won 30 games.

The Buffs' lineup included Dode Criss, a two-way star who pitched and played the field. Criss hit .348 in 1914 but did not have enough at-bats to qualify for the batting title. He also threw a no-hitter, beating Dallas 3–1 on June 20. Criss was never quite strong enough to pitch in the majors, and he didn't have a position he could play consistently well either. But he was a star in the Texas League for seven seasons, including five seasons in Houston (1913–17). Houston had one of the finest leadoff men of the era, 5-foot-6 Joe Mowry, who had started with the Buffs when they were in the South Texas League in 1905. The Buffs also had Red Davis, who led the league in stolen bases with sixty-five, and Malcolm McDonald, the league's best third baseman. The Buffs were managed by a legend of the early days of the Texas League, Pat Newnam, who played in parts of twenty seasons in the league, mostly at first base, and managed teams in San Antonio, Beaumont, and Galveston, as well as Houston, and was even an umpire in 1924.

So it was no surprise that the two best teams in the league battled down to the last day of the season. On that Labor Day, Houston led Waco by one game—both teams had the same number of losses, but the Buffs had two more victories. The Navigators could win the pennant by sweeping a doubleheader with Dallas if the Buffs split theirs with Galveston.

Waco did its part, whipping the Giants in two quick games. Houston won the first game with the Galveston Pirates but was down 2–1 going into the fifth inning of the second game. After the Pirates scored several runs in the top of the fifth, the umpires called the game because of darkness. The unfinished contest left Houston with a winning percentage of .673 to .670 for Waco, and apparently the pennant was theirs.

Waco's management obviously was upset at the umpires' decision. "Waco contended that there was bright sun at Dallas when the Houston game was reported called on account of darkness," league historian William Ruggles wrote in his 1951 book. "The meteorologists and almanac folks were called to pass on the state of sunlight. As a matter of personal opinion, the present historian, who scored the game officially at Houston, does not think the fifth inning should have been started at all. The sky was too dark for good baseball and risky with a fast-ball pitcher working. But there was as much daylight after Galveston's fifth as when the inning began."

Then Waco discovered that way back on June 26 Houston had broken a rule about the length of games in a doubleheader. With the first contest dragging and Houston leading 9–1, Austin agreed to end the game after the seventh inning to allow time to play a second contest. Baseball rules of the time, though, stated that the first game of a doubleheader had to be nine innings.

On September 7, Texas League president W.R. Davidson, newly elected to the job in the spring of 1914, threw out the result of the first game of the June 26 doubleheader but ignored the rule that required the game to be played over. In the meantime, someone had discovered that Waco had used outfielder Ernie Howard, acquired from Austin in a late-season trade, after the cutoff date for intraleague dealings. The game Howard played for the Navigators, a victory, also was wiped out.

At the league meeting on November 1, Houston withdrew its appeal of the ruling on the June 26 game. Galveston, which had appealed the premature ending of the Labor Day doubleheader, also gave up its appeal. "By another of these peculiar compromises the league seems to have been able to arrange, the pennant for

1914 was declared a tie between Waco and Houston," wrote Ruggles, who was at the meeting. Both teams were credited with records of 102–50.

One other major decision came out of the meeting: The umpires who had called the second game of the doubleheader between Houston and Galveston were fired. In a season as crazy as 1914, that too was no surprise.

=SECOND BASE=
THE NATIONAL PASTIME

=14=
THE DIXIE SERIES

THE DIXIE SERIES BEGAN AS AN INFORMAL CHALLENGE between the owners of the Texas League's Fort Worth Cats and the Southern Association's Little Rock Travelers in 1920, a battle between the champions of the two leagues for bragging rights. In 1921, the series became an official playoff, and in the ensuing years, it became one of the most followed baseball events from Georgia to Texas—and beyond as a baseball-crazy nation embraced playoff fervor at any level, from the majors on down. The *Sporting News* dubbed it the "Little World Series," and it produced some of the most dramatic games and showcased some of the most notable names in both leagues' histories.

Fort Worth, which dominated the Texas League in the 1920s, won five of the first six Dixie Series. The 1924 showdown with Memphis turned out to be a showcase for the Cats' Clarence "Big Boy" Kraft, who had hit .350 with 55 home runs during the regular season, not to mention driving in 196 runs—still a league record. Kraft topped off his amazing season by shredding Memphis pitching, including a three-homer effort in game four—and then retired. Looking to take advantage of his immense popularity in Fort Worth, the thirty-seven-year-old Kraft went into the automobile business after the season.

Fort Worth kept right on winning the next season, rolling to another Dixie Series title against the Atlanta Crackers. The Cats and the Crackers combined to attract 73,930 fans to the six games, an attendance record for the series that would never be equaled.

In 1931, one of the greatest teams in Texas League history was matched against one of the Southern Association's best, as the Houston Buffs, led by Dizzy Dean, took on the Birmingham Barons. A record crowd showed up at the Barons' Rickwood Field for a game one showdown between Dean and Ray Caldwell, a forty-three-year-old former big-leaguer. The Barons squeaked across a run for Caldwell in the eighth and went on to win the game 1–0 and the series 4–3.

In 1939, Fort Worth, which had finished last in the Texas League in 1938, got hot behind pitchers Ray Starr and Fred "Firpo" Marberry in the playoffs, beating Houston and Dallas for a shot at the Nashville Vols.

In game one, Starr did not allow an earned run in a 10–2 Fort Worth victory. Nashville won game two, but then Marberry, who had pitched in the majors from 1923 to 1936 and was surviving on off-speed pitches and guile, shut down the Vols in game three, scattering 10 hits in a 6–2 victory. Starr lost the next day, and then, after two rainouts, Nashville defeated Fort Worth 7–3 at the Vols' Sulphur Dell to move within one game of taking the series. But back in Fort Worth, Marberry was at his best. He did not allow a hit until one out in the ninth and finished with a one-hitter as the Cats won 11–0. Starr clinched the series the next day with a two-hitter. Marberry and Starr won all four games in the series for the Cats.

In 1949, Nashville and the Tulsa Oilers played another series that went down almost to the final out. Tulsa won the first two games at Nashville, but the Vols won two of three in Tulsa to send it back to Tennessee. Nashville catcher Carl Sawatski—who would later serve as president of the Texas League from 1976 to 1991—beat the Oilers with a grand slam in game six to send the series to a decisive seventh game.

Tulsa led 4–2 after three innings, but the Vols rallied for single runs in the fourth and fifth, and the game stayed tied until the bottom of the tenth. Nashville's Babe Barna led off the inning with a double, and Tulsa pitcher Walker Cress wisely walked Sawatski, who had hit a long solo homer in the fourth. Cress then hit center fielder Bob Borowski with a pitch to load the bases. Tulsa manager Al Vincent had to bring his infielders in to try to cut down Barna at the plate, but the Vols' Loyd Fogg hit a hard hopper that skipped off shortstop Harry Donabedian's arm for the game-winning single.

The next season, the Nashville Vols met the San Antonio Missions. The drama again was at Nashville's Sulphur Dell, an oddly shaped downtown ballpark that featured slopes to the outfield walls and an often-smoldering dump outside the right-field fence. San Antonio, playing in just its second Dixie Series, had rallied to tie it at three games apiece. But the Missions ran short on pitchers in game seven after starter Lou Sleater was knocked out in the second inning. Reliever Hoot Gibson came out of the game for a pinch hitter in the middle of a six-run Missions rally in the sixth that put San Antonio up 6–3.

Missions reliever Hal Hudson quickly gave up a run in the bottom of the inning, and the Vols still had the bases loaded with no outs. San Antonio manager Don Heffner had few choices left, so he went with Mexican League and border favorite Procopio Herrera, who had lost twelve games during the regular season but had pitched a complete-game victory over the Vols in game five. Herrera got a groundout from Bob Dant, a .338 hitter during the regular season, but a run scored to narrow the margin to 6–5. Then he got Paul Mauldin, who had driven in eighty-eight runs during the regular season, to fly out to shallow left. After an intentional walk to load the bases again, he got Paul Liptak, another good hitter, to fly out to left. San Antonio scored three runs in the eighth, and Herrera battled his way through the Nashville lineup in the eighth and ninth to clinch the game and the series.

The final Dixie Series was played in 1958 and was marked by controversy, storms, injuries, and illness. Four years before, in response to the 1954 Supreme Court ruling that school segregation was unconstitutional, the city of Birmingham had passed an ordinance forbidding mixed-race sporting events in the city. (A similar law in Louisiana had spurred Shreveport's departure from the Texas League in 1957, when the league decided not to force its clubs to field segregated teams for games in Louisiana.)

The teams playing for the Texas League pennant, the Austin Senators and Corpus Christi Giants, had African American players. George Troutman, the president of the National Association of Professional Baseball Leagues (known as the "National Association," the governing body of the minors), outlined the situation in a letter to all the minor-league clubs, noting that Austin would refuse to play without its black players. Corpus Christi said it would participate, but only if it could substitute white players for the blacks who could not play in Birmingham. Troutman refused to allow the switch.

Corpus Christi won the Texas League playoff—on a three-run homer by one of the team's black players, Bo Brassard.

The Giants replaced one of their African American players because he was injured, but the others did not play in games in Birmingham. The teams split the first two games in Alabama, then returned to Corpus Christi and split there as well. The fifth game was rained out on the Texas coast, sending the series back to Alabama. Conditions were no better there, with two rainouts and a postponement because of a college football game in nearby Tuscaloosa. The Birmingham Barons finally clinched the series with a Sunday day-night doubleheader. What turned out to be the final Dixie Series games attracted just 766 fans.

Besides the tacit racism, the series was tough on the players physically. Both Birmingham catchers were injured by foul tips during the series, and two Barons missed games because of strep throat. Corpus Christi's catcher was hit in the eye with a ball and required twelve stitches.

After the series, officials from both leagues outwardly were optimistic that the series would resume in 1959. But at the National Association meeting in the fall, the Southern Association voted to discontinue its playoff system, while the Texas League retained its postseason. Some of the reasons might have been economic—baseball was struggling mightily at the time, and a season bumping up against college football in the South did not make good financial sense. The integration issue also played a role, although it was never officially stated. But whatever the reason, the result was the same: the Dixie Series ended.

The champions of the Texas League and the newly reconstituted Southern League met in a best-of-seven playoff in 1967, but the series did not continue past that year.

=15=
IKE BOONE

IT DIDN'T TAKE IKE BOONE LONG TO MAKE A GOOD IMPRES-
sion in the spring of 1923. "He'll make 'em smile here this year,"
San Antonio Bears manager Bob Coleman told the *San Antonio
Light* about Boone, who was signed in the fall of 1922 with the
help of the New York Giants.

Boone came to San Antonio with a good reputation—he hit
.389 for New Orleans in 1921, and after a brief trial with the
Giants in 1922, he hit a combined a .316 for Toledo and Little
Rock. But those years were nothing compared to what he did in
the Texas League in 1923. He went 3 for 4 on opening day against
the Houston Buffs. Two weeks later, he tripled and scored the
winning run in a ninth-inning rally against Wichita Falls. The
next day, May 11, he had the kind of day against the league-leading Dallas Steers that made long-suffering San Antonio fans—
who had not seen a pennant-winning team since 1903—break out
in smiles.

In the bottom of the first, Boone tripled to deep left-center to
drive in a run (or as the *San Antonio Express* reported, he "zowied
one to the left-field fence"). In the second, with the Bears up 5–0,
he struck out. In the fourth, he whacked a ball to the deepest part
of San Antonio's League Park and raced around the bases for an

inside-the-park home run. In the fifth, with the score 11–4, he doubled in two runs. That left a single for the cycle, and he delivered one in the seventh. Just for good measure, he singled again in the eighth to top off a 5-for-6 day, as San Antonio won 21–4.

Both the *San Antonio Express* and the *Light* noted that Boone's first hit was his "daily triple." The barrel-chested outfielder from Samantha, Alabama, started the season on a triple-hitting tear, and he wound up with twenty-six, a league record.

But the hot hitting continued. The day he hit for the cycle, Boone was in the middle of a 14-game hitting streak that had included 6 multiple-hit games. On June 23, he had a 16-game streak broken in a 3–2 loss to Fort Worth, going 0 for 4 and dropping his batting average under .380. It would be the last day under that mark for Boone for the rest of the season.

Starting June 24, he went on a thirty-five-game hitting streak that stood as a Texas League record into the 1960s and still is a San Antonio team record. The previous record fell on July 26 with a 3-for-6 day against Wichita Falls, when his batting average topped out at .421. The streak was finally broken the next day in the second game of a doubleheader—but just barely. "The boys are still talking about the tough luck Boone had in the second game of the doubleheader Friday, when [Wichita Falls pitcher Rip] Wheeler stopped his consecutive games hitting record," the *Express* reported in its "Looking over the Keys with Mac" column. "Both of the times the slugger was charged with a time at bat he hit the ball over the fence and the high wind blew it back into the park, so that (Bob) Bescher could get under it. The second time Bescher had stopped, thinking it a sure homer." During the streak, Boone had 18 doubles and 72 hits, with 24 multiple-hit games. He boosted his average to .419 and all but locked up the league lead in eight offensive categories.

The Bears were not as successful, fading down the stretch as the powerful Fort Worth Cats rallied for their fourth pennant in a row. But there was one more mark for Boone to chase. The first week of September, he broke the league record for hits in a season with 227, and he eventually ran the mark to 241.

It was the last highlight in a season of highlights. Boone wound up leading the league in batting average (.402), hits (241), doubles (53), triples (26), runs batted in (135), total bases (391), slugging percentage (.652), and runs scored (134). All but one of those numbers have been topped in the ensuing eighty-plus years: the .402 batting average. Boone is the last player in Texas League history to top .400.

Boone went on to play briefly for the Boston Red Sox at the end of the 1923 season, and he spent parts of six more seasons in the majors. But his biggest success remained in the minors: he won the Triple Crown (the batting average, home run, and RBI titles) in the Pacific Coast League in 1929 and hit .372 to lead the International League in 1934, when he was thirty-seven and also serving as the manager of the team.

=16=
JAKE ATZ
AND PAUL LAGRAVE

WHEN SHREVEPORT GASSERS PITCHER GUS BONO SNARED A comebacker to the mound and threw to first to kill a seventh-inning rally in game seven of the 1919 Texas League championship series, he all but clinched the pennant for the Gassers. Shreveport went on to beat the Fort Worth Panthers 6–5, as Bono finished the game with two hitless innings, and the Gassers took the series for their first Texas League championship. But the Panthers were about ready to roar. For the next six seasons, Fort Worth dominated the Texas League like no team before or since. The Panthers (dubbed the Cats by the newspapers because the nickname fit into headlines better) had the league's best record every year from 1920 to 1925, including 109 victories in 1921 and 1924. When the league split the season in an effort to boost fan interest in 1920, 1921, 1922, 1924, and 1925, Fort Worth won both halves every time.

During that span, Panthers players led the league, at one time or another, in every offensive category, from batting average to sacrifices. Fort Worth pitchers led the league in victories every year, and one pitcher, left-hander Joe Pate, won thirty games twice.

Two men share much of the credit for building the Texas League's most dominant team: Paul LaGrave and Jake Atz.

LaGrave was working for the team as business manager in 1916 when team owner H. N. Weaver embarrassed his manager, Atz, by storming out of the stands and pulling a struggling pitcher from the game. Atz resigned, and the incident so upset Texas League president J. Walter Morris that he started looking for a new owner for the club, which had been a charter member of the league. Fort Worth businessman Will K. Stripling agreed to purchase the team but only if a suitable baseball man could be found to run it. Morris, who had played in the Texas League with LaGrave, recommended the thirty-two-year-old Missouri native, and he was given the job of business manager–secretary (the equivalent of today's general manager) with full authority over baseball operations.

LaGrave quickly established a network of baseball people around the country, people who could check out talent and recommend top players. His other big move was to bring back Atz.

Jake Atz was the perfect choice to manage the Panthers. A former big-leaguer, Atz walked with a decided limp after suffering a career-ending injury in 1909 when he was hit in the hip with a Walter Johnson fastball. His major-league experience of 209 games from 1902 to 1909 gave him the authority to run a ball club that would combine veterans and younger players. He and LaGrave thought alike when it came to players.

Atz was also a character, which went over well in a town that considered itself to be on the edge of the Wild West. He had given up a career in vaudeville to play baseball, and he was known as a master storyteller. Born in 1879 in Washington, D.C., his real name was John Jacob Zimmerman, and there are two stories about why he had his name legally changed to Atz. One is that he was tired of being at the end of the alphabet—especially on payday—for everything in the army. The other is that he didn't want to be at the end of the line on financially shaky ball clubs, where players were paid in alphabetical order. He managed the Cats for the last halves of the 1914 and 1915 seasons before Weaver hired him full-time in 1916, so he and LaGrave were well-acquainted when LaGrave was put in charge of the team.

Fort Worth finished second in 1917 and 1918, then had the best record in the league in 1919 before falling to Shreveport in the title series. LaGrave had signed a chunky first baseman named Clarence Kraft in 1918, and by the time of the 1919 title series Kraft was starting to have a major impact on the team. Nicknamed "Big Boy," Kraft came to Fort Worth with just three at-bats in the big leagues. But with the Panthers, he became one of the greatest hitters in league history. From 1918 to 1924, Kraft won a batting title, three home run titles, and two RBI titles, and he led the league in total bases three times, slugging percentage twice, and runs scored twice. In 1924, he set three league single-season records that still stand: extra-base hits (96), total bases (414), and runs batted in (196).

He was in the middle of a talented lineup that could score runs in bunches and play solid defense every day. Besides Kraft, LaGrave signed outfielder John "Ziggy" Sears, who hit .300 four times during the Cats' run of championships; big-league veteran Dugan Phelan, who had played in 402 games in the infield for the Reds and Cubs; sure-handed shortstop Bobby Stow, who had been the premier base-stealer in the league before World War I and league leader among shortstops in fielding percentage six times; and catcher Henry "Possum" Moore, who might have been the slowest man in the league but was also one of the hardest-hitting.

But as good as Fort Worth was in the field and at the plate, the Panthers' real strength might have been the pitching staff. The team's collection of topflight pitchers included Pate, who still holds the league record for best career winning percentage (.677, 195–93). Spitballer Paul Wachtel, who won a league-record 231 games in his career, won 20 or more games for five of the six championship years. Lil Stoner led the league in wins (27) and earned run average (2.65) in 1923 and jumped to the major leagues at the end of the season.

Although Stoner left the Cats after just one season, five men played all six years of the championship run: Moore, Sears, Pate, Wachtel, and Phelan. Kraft played five years before retiring, at the age of thirty-seven after his amazing 1924 season, when he hit 55 home runs and had a .350 batting average. But his place was quickly filled when LaGrave signed former big-leaguer "Big Ed" Konetchy, who had retired to Fort Worth after sixteen years in the majors. As Kraft's replacement at first base in 1925, Big Ed hit .345 and led the league in home runs with 41 and RBIs with 166.

The first pennant in the record run, in 1920, set off a celebration in downtown Fort Worth that included fans dragging Kraft out of bed. During the festivities, the slugger was stripped of his clothes "except for his unmentionables" and left to walk home through the streets. The win also led to the Dixie Series, between the champions of the Texas League and the Southern Association. The first best-of-seven series in 1920 was relatively informal, set up by LaGrave with the owners of the Little Rock club because the Texas League was in Class B and the Southern Association was Class A. But after Fort Worth won the series—and the games generated ticket revenues of $50,000, as well as national media interest—the Texas League was elevated to Class A, and the series became an institution. The only postseason series the Cats lost during their run of Texas League titles came in the 1922 Dixie Series, against Mobile.

The Panthers' domination of the Texas League ended after the Cats' 4–2 victory over Atlanta in the 1925 Dixie Series. Joe Pate signed with the Philadelphia A's, and the rest of the league caught up with the Cats' talent level. Fort Worth finished third in 1926 and fourth in 1927, and the dynasty was over.

LaGrave, who had become co-owner of the team with

Stripling, contracted tuberculosis in the late 1920s and died just before the 1929 season opener. Stripling sold the team soon afterward, and the new owner fired Atz on July 1 of that year.

It was the end of an era in the minors, as big-league teams began buying clubs and stocking them with their own young players. The number of long careers in the Texas League began to dwindle, and so did the prospects for another dynasty like the Cats'. Since 1925, no Texas League team has won more than two pennants in a row.

=17=
THE SPUDDERS

THE EAST TEXAS OIL BOOM SPAWNED THE POWERHOUSE
Corsicana Oil City Oilers in the early years of the twentieth century, and a boom twenty years later produced another unlikely member of the Texas League, a team that put together one of the best seasons in the league's first half-century—the Wichita Falls Spudders.

Oil had been discovered in the Wichita Falls area before World War I, but a big strike in nearby Burkburnett in 1918 had set off a frenzy—at one point, producing 7,500 barrels a day and drawing more than twenty thousand people to the region. Twenty trains a day ran between Burkburnett and Wichita Falls, and, as Al Parker put it in his book about the Spudders, *Baseball's Giant Killers: The Spudders of the '20s*, "nearly every Wichitan was sure some of that oil money was going to rub off on him—and soon."

The oil money allowed a group to buy the Texas League's Waco franchise and set up operations in Wichita Falls. The boomtown still had just forty thousand residents, making it the smallest city in all of Class A baseball. The ownership group, bursting with civic pride, built a five-thousand-seat stadium, Athletic Park, complete with a two-story clubhouse-dormitory beyond the right-field wall and a four-room residence for the groundskeeper. Single players could take advantage of the spartan accommodations upstairs during the season, and the building turned out to be sturdy—it survived two fires that wrecked large sections of the all-wood grandstand.

The owners also made two smart decisions when it came to baseball people. The first was hiring Walter Salm as the team's first manager. Salm, whose real last name was Salmberger, knew something about boomtowns—he had played for Corsicana in 1903–05, and had managed the team for part of the 1904 season. He had also played for Fort Worth, Houston, Galveston, and San Antonio, so he knew the league and the players.

He got the franchise off to a good start, finishing in the first division in each of his first four seasons as the town got behind the Spudders (the nickname, derived from oilfield terminology for starting an oil well and not from potatoes, had been selected in a contest in 1920). The Spudders' inability to win a championship in the early years of the 1920s was because they played in the same league as the Fort Worth Cats, whose overpowering teams had the best record in the league every year from 1919 to 1925.

Wanting to unload the franchise after the 1925 season, the Wichita Falls owners made their second good move—they sold to oilman J. Alvin Gardner. Gardner's first baseball experience had been as a batboy for the Beaumont club in the South Texas League, and he loved the game. He had established a league in Tampico, Mexico, while working for the Gulf Production Company there, and he had made enough money with his own oil company in Wichita Falls to bankroll the team.

Gardner set out to build a pennant-winning club. He traded center fielder Howard Fitzgerald to the Boston Red Sox during the 1926 season, getting outfielder Tom Jenkins, pitcher Joe Kiefer, and $5,000. When the Red Sox decided Fitzgerald didn't fit their plans, Gardner used the $5,000 to buy him back, and kept Jenkins and Kiefer. He signed veteran pitcher Carl Williams and then made him the team's manager.

THE CREOSOTE INCIDENT

The 1922 Spudders were one of the better teams in Wichita Falls' twelve-year history in the Texas League, winning 94 games and finishing second to a powerful Fort Worth team. In fact, in July and August Manager Walter Salm's team made a run at one of the league's more-impressive records, the 27-game winning streak put together by the 1902 Corsicana Oil City Oilers. The Spudders were at 24 in a row going into an August 12 game at Dallas against spitball artist Snipe Conley.

Conley, who was "grandfathered" when the spitball was outlawed, had always been tough on the Spudders, so someone from Wichita Falls resorted to a little skullduggery that afternoon. At some point early in the game, one or more of the game balls—and there were never more than a handful, anyway—fell into the wrong hands. Midway through the game, Conley began to complain about a burning sensation in his lips and mouth. Soon his mouth and tongue were red and swollen, limiting his effectiveness, and the Spudders eventually rallied for a 4–3 victory.

"Later analysis showed the balls had been 'doctored' by rubbing an odorless, colorless creosote compound into the seams," Al Parker wrote in *Baseball's Giant Killers*. "As Conley applied saliva from lips and tongue to his fingers he eventually was painfully burned all about his mouth."

As soon as the diagnosis had been made, Dallas protested to league president J. Doak Roberts. He brought together the league's owners, and they voted to forfeit the game to the Giants, ending the Spudders' streak at 24. Wichita Falls' management denied any knowledge of the "Creosote Incident," but talk around the league said that one of the Spudders' veteran pitchers had doctored the ball. But the one pitcher who was identified denied it, threatening to sue any newspaper that named him as the culprit. ★

Gardner signed Pete Lapan, a notoriously fast starter—and slow finisher—to catch the first half of the season, then bought Joe Cobb from Baltimore of the International League for the final months when Lapan began to cool off from his .350 pace at the plate. He signed Lyman Lamb, who had played in fifty-four games for the St. Louis Browns in 1920–21, to play the outfield. Jenkins turned out to be the spark that Wichita Falls needed at the plate. The power in his left-handed swing was to left field, where the prevailing winds at Athletic Park often carried fly balls over the fence. Jenkins, whose dark, brooding eyes and dark visage made him an intimidating hitter, wound up with a team-high .363 batting average and 25 home runs. He also led the league in runs scored with 147.

Gardner's 1926 club turned out to be powerful from top to bottom. Six of the Spudders' regulars hit over .300, and the team batting average was an even .300. Benefiting from the team's offense was the pitching staff—George Payne, who was 23–9; Fred Fussell, who was 21–8, and Kiefer, who was 20–9. Spitballer Tom Estell was 16–7.

The Spudders got off to a fast start, winning three games in Shreveport and two more in Fort Worth by a combined score of 47–17. Wichita Falls would stay in first place all season, and the Spudders wound up winning the pennant by fourteen games, going 102–54 in the process. Fans flocked to the little ballpark, which had been expanded to seat 8,500, and attendance for the season topped 131,000.

The championship put the Spudders in the Dixie Series against Southern Association champ New Orleans, and a crowd of 11,549—2,000 more than had showed up to see the New York Yankees and Babe Ruth when they came to town in 1924—came to the series opener. Wichita Falls won 2–0, and they triumphed in the second game 11–1. A special Missouri-Kansas-Texas Railroad train carried the team, two hundred rooters, and a brass band to New Orleans for the next two games, which the Spudders also swept. Wichita Falls merchant Gene Liepold, who billed himself as the "world's only Jewish cowboy," danced atop the Spudders' dugout after the team's 4–2 victory.

"The red carpet was rolled out for the returning champions," historian Parker wrote. "Hometown fans had made up a pennant fund of $7,500 to augment the Spudders' share of $621 each from the gate receipts." Since the series had been a sweep, Gardner actually made little money on it (at the time, players got the largest share of the receipts from the first four games of best-of-seven series), but he still made a profit for the year.

Virtually the entire season, the St. Louis Browns had been trying to buy Jenkins's contract, and each time Gardner had rejected their offers. But when the season ended, Gardner came up with a counteroffer: he would sell the entire team, including Jenkins, to the Browns. St. Louis' director of minor-league operations, L.C. McEvoy, accepted the deal.

Jenkins stayed with the Spudders through another playoff season in 1928, and Gardner helped out by running the team. But the oilman moved on after that. He was named vice president of the Texas League in 1929, and he assumed the president's office when J. Doak Roberts died on November 25. Gardner wound up being the longest-tenured president in league history, serving until 1954.

Wichita Falls was not as fortunate. The oilfields played out in the late 1920s, draining away money and fans, and the Depression hit the region hard. After a 5–1 loss to the Houston Buffs on May 20, 1932, the team packed up and left for good. The destination: Longview, in the new oil boom region of the state, east Texas. Wichita Falls has had neither oil nor the Texas League ever since.

=18=
NIGHT BASEBALL

IN THE EARLY DAYS OF THE TEXAS LEAGUE, BASEBALL UNDER electric lights was a novelty. In 1892, John McCloskey helped keep his Houston franchise afloat financially by putting on an exhibition night game—and an accompanying carnival of footraces and watermelon-eating contests—in front of one thousand curious paying customers.

Five years later, San Antonio took on Houston under temporary lights as a benefit for a San Antonio–based marching group, the Belknap Rifles, and drew an overflow crowd of 1,500.

But by 1930, minor-league owners began to think of night baseball as more than a novelty. With the Great Depression ravaging the nation—and the minors in particular—it became an economic necessity for teams to play when as many fans as possible could attend.

Lee Keyser, one of the owners of the Des Moines Demons in the Western League, announced at the winter meetings in 1929 that the team was going to play night games in 1930. The team spent $22,000—as much as some stadiums at the time were worth—to put up huge galvanized-iron light towers, and the first game under permanent lighting was played on May 2, 1930, in front of nearly twelve thousand fans. Little Rock, at the time a member of the Southern Association, was the first team in that league to play under the lights, on June 21.

Teams from the white-only Texas League were not the first to play under the lights in Texas, though. As permanent lights were going up in Iowa, the Negro Leagues' Kansas City Monarchs were playing under a slightly different setup. When the first generation of the Negro Leagues collapsed with the onset of the Depression, the Monarchs became a traveling team, crisscrossing the country with a caravan of trucks, four of which were equipped with forty-five-foot telescoping poles topped by six floodlights. The rest of the trucks carried the 250-horsepower, 110-megawatt generator that powered the system, plus the Monarchs and their equipment. The sheer novelty of night baseball and the ability to see a game at night—since the few jobs that were around during the Depression were normally day jobs—were enough to draw fans to the ballpark in small towns from coast to coast.

The first night game played in Texas under the Monarchs' lighting system was on May 5, 1930. A crowd of two thousand showed up at Waco's Katy Park to see the Monarchs beat the Waco Black Cardinals, 8–0. Two days later, the Monarchs beat the Dallas Black Giants 12–2 in front of seven thousand.

Owners in the Texas League recognized the benefits immediately and began plans for night games as well. The league's first regular-season night contest was played on June 20, 1930, at Waco's Katy Park, under a system that cost between $7,500 and $10,000 and that left some of the players grumbling but the league's ownership happy. Principal among the grumblers were the Fort Worth Cats, who were beaten 13–0 that night by a Waco team that had worked out three times under the lights before the day of the game.

"None too well satisfied with Friday night's game, the first ever played under artificial lights in the Texas League, electrical engineers were bust Saturday morning making adjustments in the lights and reflectors at Katy Park," the *Fort Worth Star-Telegram* reported. "More satisfactory illumination is hoped for tonight when the Waco and Fort Worth teams meet again." Infielders complained about not being able to follow ground balls, and outfielders said there was a dark zone fifteen to twenty feet off the ground. The *Star-Telegram* also noted that balls coming out of a left-handed pitcher's hand emerged from a light-colored sign in right field, explaining in part the thirteen Cats strikeouts.

Adjustments were made, and the games went on. Shreveport was the next to hold a night game in the Texas League, with a reported crowd of 4,000 seeing a game July 10. Houston spent $25,000 for a system at Buff Stadium, and 12,000 showed up on July 22. Two days later, San Antonio turned on the lights for a game with Shreveport in front of 3,400 at League Park, prompting an almost-poetic commentary by *San Antonio Express* sports editor Fred Mosebach: "The soft glow from the milk-colored Mazda lights that are strung in clusters 60 feet overhead, nestling in giant reflectors bearing a resemblance to porcelain bath tubs, lends an entrancing effect, and the scene becomes an animated picture pleasing to the eye and restful to the mind as the players dart hither and yon on the greensward like so many tots in a romp."

By the end of the season, a reported thirty-eight teams in fourteen leagues across the nation were playing at a least part of their schedules at night. The move kept more than a few teams afloat through the Depression, and it even prompted the majors to begin playing night games. It was nearly five years before the first major-league night game was played, on May 24, 1935, in Cincinnati.

=19=
GENE RYE

GENE RYE WAS AN UNLIKELY LOOKING POWER HITTER WITH
an equally unlikely nickname: Half Pint. Just 5 foot 6 and 165
pounds, Rye was small, even by standards of the late 1920s and
early 1930s when he passed through the Texas League. Rye wasn't
even his real name—he was born Eugene Mercantelli in Chicago
in 1906—although he is listed as Rye in virtually all baseball refer-
ences. A newspaper article in 1932 said that Gene and his brother
Billy were dubbed "rye bread," later shortened to just Rye, by semipro teammates because of their dark complexions.

Gene Rye had been signed by the Waco Cubs on the recom-
mendation of Stump Eddington, a former Texas Leaguer who in
1928 was managing a team in the Class C Piedmont League. "He
will hit more home runs at Katy Park than I ever could," was
Eddington's report, as noted in the *Waco Times-Herald*. Rye hit
.289 with 12 homers and 68 RBIs in 122 games for Winston-
Salem in 1928.

Katy Park—which was the first Texas League ballpark to get
lights, on June 20, 1930—was nestled next to Baylor Stadium and
the Cotton Palace Fair Grounds on what at the time was the edge
of Waco. The fences, especially in right field, were tall but close, and
Eddington knew that the left-handed-hitting Rye could reach them

on a regular basis. He didn't get much of a chance early in 1929, but after a slow start he hit 19 homers and drove in 53 runs in 129 games. He began to show signs of the promise Eddington had predicted early the next season, when, 4 games into the schedule, he went 5 for 6 with 3 home runs in a 15–5 romp over San Antonio.

His big offensive day wasn't all that uncommon in a year when thirteen Texas Leaguers would have 100 or more runs batted in and just two pitchers would win 20 games. But what Rye did on the night of August 6, 1930, would set him apart from the rest of the league.

Waco trailed Beaumont 6–2 going into the bottom of the eighth inning, and Exporters pitcher Gerald Mallett was headed toward what looked like an easy complete-game victory. Leading off the inning, Rye ripped a pitch from Mallett down the right-field line, a ball that just curved foul. But on the next delivery, he drove an outside pitch over the left-field wall to make it 6–3. Two walks and a single later, Mallett was gone, and Guy Green was pitching in relief for the Exporters. Green gave up a run-scoring single, walked in a run, allowed a two-run double, walked another, and then gave up a two-run single, as Waco took the lead, 9–6.

Walter Newman, referred to as the "sheik of Cuero" by the Waco newspaper, came into the game to face Rye. "The squatty outfielder waded into a fast one," the *Waco Times-Herald* reported. "He is little, but at bat he has the power of a giant. His big bat is T.N.T to opposing pitchers. When he starts exploding homers, there's only one remedy, and that's a base on balls. It was not offered last night." The three-run homer made it 12–6, and Beaumont still hadn't recorded an out. Newman finally was able to retire a batter, Charlie Stuvengen, on a fly ball. But an error and another home run pushed the lead to 14–6. Newman struck out Bob Sanguinet, but then a walk, a throwing error, a run-scoring single, another single, and a walk loaded the bases as Rye came to the plate for the third time.

"Here was the opportunity of the half-pint star to get several records unequalled in the long history of the game," the *Times-Herald* reported. Rye worked the count to 1–2, then fouled off a pitch. Newman threw him a curveball—a pitch Rye apparently was looking for—and the little outfielder hit it on a line over the right-field wall for a grand slam. It gave him three home runs and eight RBIs in the inning. "Some of those present had been witnessing baseball games since they wore knee-pants, and now had flowing white locks or no locks at all, yet they had never seen the like of Rye's performance on the diamond," the *Times-Herald* said.

Stuvengen followed Rye with a solo homer to top off the 18-run inning, the second-biggest explosion in league history. The record is 19, set on June 29, 1896, by the Fort Worth Panthers against the Galveston Sand Crabs. And while Waco's 18-run inning isn't a record, Rye's 3 homers and 8 RBIs in the inning are still unmatched. He is also the last player in league history to score 3 runs in an inning.

After two seasons in which he hit 45 home runs in the Texas League, Rye got his shot at the majors in 1932. But he played in just 17 games for the Boston Red Sox and had just 7 hits—all singles.

=20=
DIZZY DEAN

DIZZY DEAN WAS THE MOST FAMOUS 1–0 PITCHER IN BIG-league baseball in the spring of 1931. He had gone a combined 26–10 in three leagues in 1930, including a three-hit shutout of the Pittsburgh Pirates in his major league debut on September 28. He had dominated hitters in the Western League, going 17–8 for St. Joseph, Missouri, and he was 8–2 for Houston in the Texas League.

But it was his personality that landed him on the sports pages from New York to St. Louis to Los Angeles. Dean was a free spirit before the phrase was invented, a quotation machine for writers looking for an angle. He asked to be called "The Great Dean" in stories and predicted he would win 25 games for the Cardinals (because saying he would win 30 "would be bragging"). In February, he was featured in a half-page article in the *Sporting News*, at the time the national baseball newspaper.

The St. Louis Cardinals, who had signed Dean off the Public Services Utilities semipro team in San Antonio in 1929, had tried to keep him out of trouble during the off-season, with little success. Turned loose in Bradenton, Florida, the Cardinals' spring-training home, early in 1931, Dean went on a spending spree. He bought clothes and cigars, sodas by the case, sunglasses, and stationery. He came close to chartering a boat for a weekend fishing trip before Cardinals vice president Branch Rickey arrived in Florida.

Writing bad checks—or signing Rickey's name on them— Dean ran up more than $2,700 in bills in the Bradenton area. Rickey was apoplectic. Dean's response: "Take it outta my pay." Rickey estimated that Dean had spent his way well into his 1932 salary, but the Cardinals paid off the bills and put Dean on a dollar-a-day budget as training camp opened. Dean responded by picking up on the field where he had left off the summer before. In an exhibition game against the world champion Philadelphia A's, he allowed a leadoff double to start his inning of work, then struck out the side on 10 pitches.

Dean's immodest ways irritated the veterans in the Cardinals' camp and did little to endear him to St. Louis manager Gabby Street. He was with the big-league team when the season opened, but Street didn't even warm him up the first two weeks of the season. On May 2, Dean was told he was going back to Houston. "Rickey said Dean still was the best pitcher on his staff, but he wanted to send him [to Houston] because Joe Schultz, Houston manager, knows how to handle him," the Associated Press reported.

Upon hearing the news, Dean raced to the Western Union office and sent a collect telegram to Schultz, telling him he would be ready to start the next day. He arrived in Houston at 2 P.M. on May 3. That night, he beat Wichita Falls 6–0 with a three-hitter.

The next time he pitched, it was in front of a crowd of twelve thousand. He shut out Shreveport on four hits. The next night, he threw three innings of shutout ball in relief and doubled in the winning run in the bottom of the eleventh as Houston beat Dallas.

He jumped into the national headlines again on May 17 when he tangled with Dallas catcher Al Todd after a brushback pitch.

Todd got the better of the fight, but Houston won the game 7–1. "Well, it looks like the ol' master of the mound can catch 'em, too," Dean said afterward, rubbing a sore jaw. "That guy Todd is almost as good fightin' as me pitchin'. So that makes us even—he won the fight and I won the game." The story went out on the wire services:

> DALLAS, TEXAS—Dizzy Dean, eccentric and youthful pitcher who was banished to Houston by the Cardinals, won a nicely pitched ball game here today, but lost a popular boxing decision to Alfred Todd, husky Dallas catcher.

Dean won his fifth straight, a 2–0 shutout of San Antonio, on June 3 and announced afterward that he was getting married. Although Houston president Fred Ankenman and Rickey weren't thrilled at the idea—and wouldn't let Dean have the ceremony at home plate—the marriage turned out to be good for the flaky pitcher. Pat Dean wound up managing his finances and many aspects of his life for the next forty-three years.

On June 29, Dean pitched and won both ends of a double-header against Fort Worth. The next night, he relieved in the first inning and pitched eight more innings, went 4 for 4 at the plate, and even stole a base.

As Dean's legend grew, attendance soared all over the league. The Buffs wound up averaging a league-best 3,000 fans a game, but when Dean pitched, the crowds swelled to between 8,000 and 14,000. Around the league, teams that were drawing in the hundreds would draw six times as many fans if word got out that Dean was pitching.

When the first half of the season ended in July, Houston and Beaumont were tied at 50–30. The Buffs won a special best-of-three series for the top spot, and rumors flew that Dean would be headed for St. Louis. But Rickey told the Houston papers that the Cardinals, who were on their way to the pennant, didn't need him.

Dean just got stronger. He struck out 12 Wichita Falls batters on August 17. He struck out 13 against Shreveport on September 1. He struck out 16 and gave up just 4 hits against Beaumont on September 4. Not surprisingly, the Buffs ran away with the second half, finishing 14 games ahead of Beaumont and claiming the pennant, and with it a trip to the Dixie Series against Birmingham.

Fans from all over the South lined up at the Barons' Rickwood Field for game one of the series, which matched Dean and the Barons' forty-three-year-old ace, Raymond "Old Man" Caldwell. Caldwell, who had pitched in the big leagues before Dean was born, was 19–7 for the Barons in 1931, getting by on his experience.

The two pitchers put on a game for the ages. Caldwell pitched out of trouble in every inning and Dean mowed through the Barons, with neither team able to score until the bottom of the eighth. With two away, Birmingham got two singles and a double against Dean to score the only run Caldwell needed. He retired the Buffs in order in the ninth.

Houston won the next three games, including a 2–0 win on Dean's three-hitter in game four. But the Barons rallied to take the next two contests and send the series to game seven in Houston.

"Them Barons didn't see me at my best in the daytime, no foolin'," Dean said before the night game. "Nighttime is my time to shine." The showdown went into the eighth tied at 2–2, but the Barons scored when the Houston center fielder, future Hall of Famer Joe "Ducky" Medwick, let a ball roll through his legs. Birmingham scored three more times in the ninth to put the game away and claim the series, which veteran umpire Ziggy Sears called "the best Dixie Series ever."

In a runaway vote, Dean was named the most valuable player in the Texas League. He had gone 26–10 and had led the league in wins, complete games (28), shutouts (11), and strikeouts (303). He was second in ERA at 1.57.

He went on to a Hall of Fame career, including a 30-win season in 1934. But a broken toe suffered in the 1937 All-Star game started him on a slide that would eventually end his career. He was traded to the Chicago Cubs before the 1938 season, and in 1940 he volunteered to go to Tulsa of the Texas League to try to work his way back.

Dean drew big crowds all over the league when he returned—including an overflow mob of more than twelve thousand in San Antonio—but he was not the Dean of old. Surviving on curveballs and moxie, he went 8–8 in twenty-one games for the Oilers, his career all but over.

He began a second career soon afterward, and his folksy style of play-by-play endeared him to another generation of baseball fans. He worked in the radio and television booths into the 1960s.

=21=
ED COLE
AND DAVE WILHELMI

A PERFECT GAME, RETIRING ALL TWENTY-SEVEN HITTERS without allowing a base runner, is one of the rarest feats in baseball. In the history of Major League Baseball, just thirteen pitchers have thrown perfect games.

Some of the big-leaguers who threw perfect games, such as Sandy Koufax and Catfish Hunter, are in the Baseball Hall of Fame. Some are noteworthy because of the circumstances, like Don Larsen, who pitched a perfect game in the 1956 World Series. But most of them had otherwise ordinary careers, and their perfect games became footnotes to history. Such is the case with the two players who pitched perfect games in the history of the Texas League. The first was thrown during the Depression by a pitcher in the early stages of a twenty-year career in professional baseball. The second, forty-eight years later, was turned in by a pitcher who played just six seasons and never progressed beyond the Texas League.

Ed Cole—who was born Edward William Kisleauskas in Wilkes-Barre, Pennsylvania, on March 22, 1909—was in his fourth season of professional baseball in 1935. He had stayed close to home his first three years, playing for Johnstown, Pennsylvania, in the Middle Atlantic League and Wilkes-Barre and Hazelton,

Pennsylvania, in the New York–Penn League. But in 1935, coming off an 18–13 season for Hazelton, he joined the Galveston Buccaneers of the Texas League. The Buccaneers had won the pennant the year before, the city's first in the twentieth century, and they had a solid club again in 1935.

The night of July 10, the Tulsa Oilers were in Galveston for a night game at Moody Stadium, and Cole was scheduled to pitch against Ed Selway, who was in his third season with the Oilers.

Cole was sharp from the start, and by the sixth inning the crowd was aware that he had not allowed a base runner. With one away in that inning, Cole went to a full count on Heine Mueller, the Oilers' shortstop, and the crowd gasped when Mueller started for first after the pitch. But umpire Frank Coe's right fist shot up, and Mueller was called out on strikes. In the eighth, Cole got behind in the count to first baseman Art Shoap with three straight balls. But the right-hander came back to pitch strikes, including a called third strike to retire Shoap and end the inning.

While Cole was shutting down the Oilers, Selway was doing the same to the Bucs. Galveston first baseman Bill McGhee led off the fifth with a triple, but the Bucs couldn't get him in, even with an attempted double steal (Tulsa threw to third to hold him to the base when the runner from first broke for second). Galveston's Fred Frink circled the bases in the eighth after Selway fielded his bunt and threw the ball away, far down the right-field line. But Frink was sent back to second on a ground rule, and he was left on base after Selway got a groundout and a popup to end the inning.

Cole retired the first two batters in the top of the ninth, but his first pitch to Selway was so wild that catcher Bob Linton couldn't even get a glove on it. Linton, who was also Galveston's manager, calmed his pitcher down, and Cole came back to get a strikeout. In the bottom of the inning, Selway was one out away from extra innings when his nemesis on the day came up: McGhee, who already was 2 for 3 against him. McGhee, perhaps not wanting to take a chance on sending the game to extra innings, swung away at the fist pitch and whacked it to the deepest part of the park. He took off for first and never slowed down, barely sliding around catcher Gus Brittain's lunging tag for an inside-the-park home run to win the game.

Brittain, disgusted at the fact that he had slightly juggled the relay throw, was left on his knees at the plate as the Bucs mobbed McGhee. "Later he raised himself to his feet and heaved the ball high over the grandstand, apparently heartbroken that he hadn't been able to grasp the ball more quickly and save the score against the stout-hearted Ed Selway," the *Galveston News* reported. "It was that kind of a baseball game."

Cole struck out eight that night, and he finished the season 15–19, with a 3.24 ERA, as the Bucs made the postseason for the second year in a row. He went on to pitch two more seasons with Galveston before getting his shot at the major leagues. In 1938, he was 1–5 for the St. Louis Browns, and in 1939, after going 16–10 for San Antonio, he got his last shot at the majors. Returning to the Browns, he was 0–2 in six appearances. Cole proved to be a durable minor-league pitcher, however, and he played until 1951, appearing for clubs in seven different leagues. He finally retired after going 4–12 for Port Arthur in the Gulf Coast League at the age of forty-two.

Dave Wilhelmi's career came in a different era, and it took a different path. He was a big (6 foot 5 and 230 pounds) hard-throwing right-hander who was in his fourth pro season in 1983. In his first three years, he compiled a combined 24–38 record in two levels of Class A, and he had been on the disabled list for two weeks before getting just his second start of the season for the Shreveport Captains against the Arkansas Travelers on the night of May 3. The twenty-one-year-old Wilhelmi hadn't pitched well for the Captains even when he wasn't injured. Going into the game, he was 0–1 with an ERA of well over 7.00.

But Shreveport got him a lead early in the game, which allowed him to pitch more aggressively. The Captains scored a run in the second and four in the fourth, then added single runs in the sixth and eighth. Wilhelmi didn't have any close calls until the bottom of the eighth, when he went to a 3–0 count on the Travelers' Ron Hunt before throwing a strike and getting a fly ball to right.

In the ninth, Greg Guin hit a fly ball to left-center that looked like it had a chance to fall in. But left fielder Don Mazzilli made a diving catch for the first out. Larry Reynolds then hit a sinking liner to right field, but Rob Deer charged in and made a sliding catch. Those were two of just five outs by the Captains' outfield. The next batter was Larry Reynolds, who had been thrown out on the closest infield play of the game, in the bottom of the sixth. Reynolds flied out to shallow right, and the crowd of 1,761 cheered the visiting pitcher as his teammates mobbed him. "I don't even realize what I've done," Wilhelmi told the *Arkansas Democrat*. "I'll probably realize it tomorrow."

The perfect game turned out to be the highlight of Wilhelmi's short professional career. He had a record of 9–8 for the Captains in 1983 but was 5–11 the next year and 0–3 with an 8.25 ERA for Fresno in 1985, his final season in professional baseball.

=22=
ALL-STAR GAMES

IN THE SUMMER OF 1933, AS PART OF CHICAGO'S CENTURY OF Progress Exposition, Major League Baseball put on its first All-Star game. The lineups were studded with some of the greatest players of all time—including Babe Ruth, who hit the game's first home run—and the contest featured two of the sport's greatest managers, Connie Mack and John McGraw.

Three years later, the Texas League had its own excuse for what the newspapers called a "dream" game: the Texas Centennial celebration in Dallas. As with the majors, the lineups were filled with some of the league's greatest players, including Paul Easterling, who played in the league thirteen seasons, and Homer Peel, who hit .325 in parts of fourteen seasons. An enthusiastic crowd of ten thousand showed up at Dallas' Steer Park for the game on July 25, 1936, spurring the league to announce that the game would become an annual affair.

The owners let the fans vote on the rosters, and they responded by picking some of the league's most notable names. They also got to pick the managers, choosing Galveston's Jake Atz, who had led Fort Worth's dynasty of the 1920s, and Oklahoma City's Bert Niehoff, whose club had won the Dixie Series the year before. Every club in the eight-team league had tickets, and they sold fast.

The fans who filled Steer Stadium—on the night of the state's Democratic primary—saw Atz's team (made up of players from Galveston, San Antonio, Houston, and Beaumont) beat the Niehoff team (with players from Oklahoma City, Dallas, Fort Worth, and Tulsa), 4–2.

"With this turnout and display of enthusiasm that brought fans here from all points in the circuit, the game was stamped a huge success," the *Dallas Morning News*' George White reported. League president J. Alvin Gardner announced after the game that it would become an annual affair, and cities from around the league began to offer to host it. Houston, with one of the league's bigger parks, landed the game in 1937.

Fan interest also grew, with more than 110,000 ballots cast for the rosters. Ed Cole, who had thrown the league's first perfect game in 1935, started for the South, but it was his team's second pitcher of the night who got the headlines. Houston's John Grodzicki came into the game in the fourth inning and struck out the first six batters he faced, all of them .300 hitters: Homer Peel, Red Harvel, Joe Bilgere, Lou Brower, Norman McCaskill, and Ed "Bear Tracks" Greer. As the papers of the day noted, it was comparable to the New York Giants' Carl Hubbell striking out five in a row in the 1934 All-Star game.

With Houston sitting in seventh place, the Buffs' owners were worried about the turnout for the game. But an overflow crowd of more than eight thousand showed up, ensuring that the midseason game would continue.

Over the years, the game has gone through a variety of formats. In the first contest, the league's eight teams were split into north and south squads. In some years, the first-place club played the rest of the league. In others, the league's all-stars played one of Texas' major-league clubs. Six times, the Texas League's best played the Mexican League's all-stars. Today, the stars are chosen from the league's East and West divisions.

And while not all the all-star games have matched the first one's attraction, there have been some memorable contests through the years. The first game, besides serving as part of the state's centennial celebration, was also seen as a way to boost interest in the Texas League during the Depression. League-wide attendance had dropped to 522,512 in 1933, just seven years after the league's teams had drawn 1,159,905 fans. Teams were struggling to bring people back into the ballparks and get them talking about the league again.

In 1940, the North won in eleven innings. After the war, interest boomed again as the all-stars took on the league's first-place club from 1947 to 1949. But in the late 1950s, with attendance sagging, the league arranged an interlocking schedule with the Mexican League, called the Pan American Association, and a new format for the midseason game. There would be two games, one on each side of the border.

The first interleague all-star game was played in Mexico City on July 12, 1959. Despite problems with promoting the contest— the Mexico City club official in charge of publicity was fired early in July—the game drew a crowd of 19,089 to El Parque Deportivo de Seguro Social. Although not reaching the reaching the league's expectations of pushing the stadium record of 30,000, the turnout is still the biggest in the history of Texas League All-Star games. The Mexican-Leaguers won, 9–3.

In 1960 the Texas League stars exacted a measure of revenge with a 7–3 win in front of more than 8,000 fans at San Antonio's Mission Stadium. Hoping to capitalize on the popularity of the event, the two leagues agreed to have two all-star games in 1961, with games on both sides of the border. The Mexican all-stars swept both contests—8–3 at Mexico City on July 16 before a crowd of more than 14,000, and 12–3 on July 30 at San Antonio. Luis Tiant was credited with the win in the second game. The future major league star struck out six in three innings of work.

The series would not continue past 1961. When the two leagues failed to renew the Pan American Association agreement, inter-league play was scuttled, and so was the all-star format.

The game returned to a north-versus-south format in 1962, but in 1963, the league came up with a new arrangement—the Texas League stars took on the National League's Houston Colt .45s in San Antonio, home of the Colts' farm club. An overflow crowd of 8,816 showed up at Mission Stadium to see the first appearance of a major-league club in the city since the 1940s, and the partisan crowd almost went home disappointed.

The game went to the bottom of the ninth tied at 3–3, and the Texas League team had run out of pitchers. "League President Dick Butler was gnawing his nails, as it appeared the game might go into extra innings with no more pitchers left on the Texas League bench," the *Sporting News* reported. Colts pitcher Dick Drott walked Austin's Sandy Alomar to start the ninth, and after Alomar was bunted to second, he stole third. Two more walks loaded the bases for Tulsa's Jim Beauchamp. Beauchamp, in the middle of a monster season that saw him hit 31 homers and drive in 105 runs, ripped the first pitch from Drott over the wall in left-center for a game-winning grand slam, the first time the game had been decided in such dramatic fashion.

Some of the all-star contests were noteworthy not for the game itself but for the personalities involved. At Alexandria, Louisiana, in 1972, four Baseball Hall of Famers were involved in the contest between the all-stars and the Texas Rangers: Rangers manager Ted Williams and first-base coach Nellie Fox, Alexandria manager Duke Snider, and Rangers broadcaster Don Drysdale. Stan Wasiak, who went on to set the record for most games won as a minor-league manager, was the comanager of the Texas League squad. Rangers shortstop Toby Harrah earned mention for a different reason that year: he was stricken with appendicitis during batting practice and was in surgery when the game began.

In 1974, Rangers manager Billy Martin decided to have a little fun with the game against the all-stars. Martin, who had retired as a player in 1961, played second base in the seventh inning. First-base coach Jackie Moore caught the last three innings. Charlie Silvera, forty-nine years old and another member of Martin's staff, pinch-ran in the ninth. Utility man Duke Sims played seven different positions for the Rangers. But of all the players who got into the game—and Martin played virtually everyone, including his staff—perhaps the most noteworthy was the all-stars' starting pitcher: future Hall of Famer Dennis Eckersley, who gave up two runs in two innings of the all-stars' 10–5 victory.

In 1981, with the all-stars playing league-leading Tulsa at the Drillers' Sutton Stadium, Tulsa's Marty Scott played all nine positions. He started out at catcher and wound up on the mound, striking out San Antonio's Mike Zouras in the ninth inning of a tie game with the go-ahead run at third base. The all-stars went on to win 9–5 in ten innings.

A player who wasn't even selected to the game in 1984—hosted by Jackson, Mississippi—had its most dramatic hit. Jackson Mets outfielder Billy Beane, who had to be tracked down in Birmingham, Alabama, the morning of the game, hadn't been chosen to the East all-stars by the managers, but he was next in line. When Tulsa outfielder Bob Brower was promoted to Triple-A, the call went out for Beane. And then another and another. Jackson Mets general manager Mike Feder finally found the center fielder at a Birmingham Barons game, and Beane hustled back to Jackson for that night's game.

Going into the bottom of the ninth, Beane had done nothing at the plate—he was 0 for 4 and had struck out against El Paso's Teddy Higuera in his previous at-bat. The East trailed 7–6 after blowing a 6–2 lead. But Beane's Jackson teammate Al Pedrique started the ninth with a single, and one out later Beane came up. He took the first pitch for a ball, but he was ready for the second, a high changeup. He hit it over the wall in dead center field for a game-winning home run.

Beane made his big-league debut later that season, playing in 5 games for the New York Mets. He wound up playing 148 games in an undistinguished major-league career but went on to fame as a general manager, turning the low-budget Oakland Athletics into a consistent winner with a combination of savvy scouting and strong player development.

Jackson was the scene of another dramatic finish, this time in 1992, when the East rallied for seven runs in the bottom of the ninth for an 8–6 victory. Shreveport's Adell Davenport capped the enormous inning with a two-out, two-run homer off Wichita's Mark Ettles. Ettles, the last pitcher available to West manager Bruce Bochy, gave up four hits and all seven runs in two thirds of an inning. The outburst was the most runs ever scored in the ninth inning in the game's history, and the comeback was the biggest ever.

The next season, the managers agreed before the game to play only nine innings, no matter what the score was. Officially, the game at Wichita's Lawrence-Dumont Stadium ended in a 3–3 tie. Unofficially, the East won on a homer-hitting contest when Arkansas' Darrel Deak curled a ball around the right-field foul pole on his third try. Wichita's Dwayne Hosey, who was the game's most valuable player (MVP) after hitting two homers in the game, failed to connect in three tries.

In 1994, the Texas and Mexican leagues revived their series after thirty-three years, playing on June 12 in Monterrey and June 13 at San Antonio's brand-new Municipal Stadium. In front of nineteen thousand fans, the Mexican-Leaguers won the contest at Monterrey Stadium, 4–3, on a ninth-inning triple by Daniel Fernandez and a two-out single by Adam Casillas. The Texas Leaguers won the next night, 5–1. That game also helped a former San Antonio Dodgers pitcher get back to the major leagues, as Fernando Valenzuela showed he still had his stuff—he was pitching for the Philadelphia Phillies less than a month later and went on to play for the San Diego Padres 1995–97 and the St. Louis Cardinals for part of the 1997 season. The international series was played again in 1995 and 2000.

The all-star game has not been back to its original Dallas location since 1957—the city hasn't been a part of the league since 1971—but the contest will return to the area in 2005 when the Dallas suburb of Frisco, which joined the league in 2003, will host it for the first time.

=23=
HANK OANA

HENRY KAUHANE OANA HAD ALREADY BEEN TO THE MAJOR
leagues when he signed with the Fort Worth Cats for the 1942
season, and he had a nickname, Prince, stuck on him in San
Francisco, where someone had gotten the mistaken impression
that he was related to the Hawaiian royal family.

He had also proved himself as a strong hitter, leading the
Arizona State League in batting in his first season as a pro, in
1929, and hitting .345 for San Francisco in 1931 and .332 for
Portland in 1933. He topped one hundred RBIs in back-to-back
seasons for Jackson in the Southeastern League in 1938–39. But
Fort Worth manager Rogers Hornsby was interested in Prince
Oana for another reason: his arm. Oana, whose big-league career
up to that point had consisted of six games in the outfield for the
1934 Phillies, was willing to try something new. So Hornsby—the
former big-leaguer who was elected to the Baseball Hall of Fame
in 1942—made Oana a pitcher.

The experiment worked. In June, the thirty-two-year-old
Hawaiian threw a twelve-inning shutout for the Cats, allowing
the Houston Buffs eight hits but no runs. "By outlasting young
Eldred Byerly and shading Elmer Rummans, the veteran Hank
Oana gave strong evidence that his transformation from an
outfielder to a pitcher has been not only complete and successful

but a positive stroke of genius," Flem Hall wrote in the *Fort Worth Star-Telegram*. "No pitcher in the league could have done a better job than Oana did against the Buffs."

Oana hurled another gem just two weeks later. Pitching in the seven-inning second game of a July 4 doubleheader, he no-hit the Dallas Rebels. Just two Rebels reached base, both in the bottom of the first. "From then on not a Rebel reached base, as Hank kept his fast one under the Dallas players' chins and demonstrated a fine change of pace when he had to," Flint Dupre reported in the *Dallas Morning News*.

Oana wound up at 16–5 with a 1.72 earned run average for the Cats in 1942, earning a trip to the majors the next year as a pitcher. He was 3–2 in seven games for the Detroit Tigers in 1943 and made three appearances for the Tigers in 1945.

He reappeared in the Texas League in 1946, this time with Dallas. At the age of thirty-eight, he led the league in wins (24, with 10 losses), complete games (27), and innings pitched (284) and was named the Pitcher of the Year. He also was the only Dallas hitter with more than 100 at-bats who hit better than .300. During the regular season, the Fort Worth bench jockeys rode him hard as one of Dallas's "worn out old men," but Oana beat the Cats three times, including a ten-inning, two-hit shutout on July 4.

In the postseason, pitching on instinct as much as natural ability, he won three times. He threw a five-hitter to beat San Antonio 4–0, clinching the first-round series. Then he stopped Fort Worth 6–2 in game four, helping Dallas to a 4–1 series victory and the Texas League pennant. In the Dixie Series, Oana gave up ten hits but just three runs in a 13–3 victory over Atlanta in game one, getting a bases-loaded strikeout to end the game. Dallas went on to win the series, the city's first Dixie Series title since 1926.

Prince Oana ended his career in the Class B Big State League, where he pitched and managed teams until 1951. He died in Austin in 1976.

=24=
THE 1942 PLAYOFFS

IN THE FALL OF 1942 NOTHING WAS OFFICIAL YET, BUT THERE
was a feeling around the Texas League that the Shaughnessy
playoffs might be the last ones for a while. (The Shaughnessy
system was devised by International League executive Frank
Shaughnessy during the Depression to boost fan interest. Under
his plan, the first-place team in the league at the end of the regular season played the fourth-place team, the second- and third-
place teams met, and the winners in the first round played for the
championship.)

The United States had been engaged in World War II for just
over ten months. Although President Franklin D. Roosevelt had
written to Commissioner Kenesaw Mountain Landis to encourage the majors to continue playing, the minors were a different
story. Many minor-league owners remembered 1918, when virtually every league shut down for World War I, some as early as June
of that year. Limitations on travel were coming, and the draft
already was starting to take minor-leaguers. So there was a sense
of finality when fourth-place San Antonio opened the postseason
against regular-season leader Beaumont and third-place Fort
Worth traveled to second-place Shreveport.

The Fort Worth Cats were managed by Rogers Hornsby, four

years removed from a playing career that would land him in the Baseball Hall of Fame. Hornsby was managing his second team in the Texas League; he had started the 1941 season at Oklahoma City in 1941 but had "resigned" in late June after a disappointing 31–37 start. Fort Worth hired Hornsby to replace Bob Linton, who had led the Cats to fourth-, fifth- and eighth-place finishes from 1939 to 1941. The Cats' management hoped that Hornsby, who was known to be a tough, no-nonsense baseball man, would be able to return the club to the level of dominance it had enjoyed in the 1920s.

The Shreveport Sports were managed by Francis "Salty" Parker, who had played his first year in the minors at seventeen and at twenty-nine was already in his fourth season as a manager. He had taken Shreveport to the playoffs in 1941 and 1942 after leading Lubbock to the West Texas–New Mexico League pennant in 1939 and Marshall to the East Texas League postseason in 1940. Shreveport president Bonneau Peters had also assured Parker that he would have a job in 1943—if there were any jobs to be handed out.

Shreveport won the first two games of the best-of-seven series at home, beating 16-game-winner Hank Oana in the opener and 21-game-winner Earl Caldwell the next night. But the Cats' Claud Horton gave up just 5 hits when the series resumed at Fort Worth's LaGrave Field, and the Cats won 2–1. Fort Worth evened the series at two games apiece the next afternoon behind Oana, winning again by the score of 2–1.

That set up a duel between Caldwell and 19-game winner Ralph "Bruz" Hamner, the ace of Shreveport's staff. But Caldwell and Hamner were long gone when game five was decided after four hours and twenty-two minutes of what *Fort Worth Star-Telegram* writer Bill Van Fleet described as a "bitter and colorful battle" in front of 4,703 fans. Caldwell, his right foot shot full of painkillers after it had been spiked, pitched the first seven innings for the Cats, allowing three unearned runs. Hamner gave up two runs in the bottom of the seventh, then a game-tying triple to pinch hitter Merv Connors in the eighth.

That was the way it stayed for the next ten innings, although both teams had chances to end it sooner. Shreveport loaded the bases in the ninth, but Cats center fielder Zeke Trent threw out Sports pitcher Floyd Speer trying to score on a sacrifice fly. Speer tried to run over Cats catcher Ronnie Ronaldson on the play. As a result of the collision, Ronaldson suffered a gash under his eye, but he held on to the ball.

Fort Worth got leadoff doubles in the twelfth, thirteenth, and fourteenth innings but couldn't get the runners home. Shreveport could get nothing going against Horton, who had come into the game with a man on first in the ninth, until leadoff man Sonny Sonnier led off the nineteenth with a slow roller down the third-base line. Connors, who had led the league in home runs and extrabase hits in 1942 but had struggled in the field, couldn't make a play on the ball, and Sonnier had his fourth hit of the night. He was sacrificed to second, but the next Shreveport hitter struck out. That left it to Joe Cavosie, who was hitless in his last four at-bats. This time, the Sports' right fielder delivered, grounding a single to right. Sonnier beat the throw to the plate for the game's first run since the eighth. In the home half of the nineteenth, the Sports' Al Bronkhurst retired the Cats to clinch the victory.

The contest is among the longest in Texas League history, and it remains the longest playoff game. Fort Worth tied the series when it resumed the next night in Shreveport, as Oana blanked the Sports 1–0. But Shreveport knocked out Horton early the next game and then bombed Oana to win, 8–2, and claim the first-round series.

Shreveport went on to beat Beaumont—which had taken its series with San Antonio the night of the nineteen-inning marathon in Fort Worth—four games to three. It was Shreveport's first Texas League title since beating Fort Worth in a playoff in 1919.

The playoffs turned out to be the league's last games for more than three years, as the league's directors voted at their annual meeting to suspend operations for the duration of the war. Many of the stars of the 1942 playoffs returned to the league when play resumed in 1946, among them Oana, Caldwell, and Connors. Parker came back to manage the Sports, although they never won another pennant for him. Hornsby returned to the league in 1950, leading Beaumont to the league's best regular-season record.

=25=
BOBBY BRAGAN

BOBBY BRAGAN WAS SITTING IN THE BROOKLYN DODGERS' dugout at Ebbets Field one June afternoon in 1948. As usual, he wasn't playing that day—thirty-year-old third-string catchers hitting .167 didn't get into many games. For backstops, the Dodgers also had twenty-five-year-old Bruce Edwards, who had hit .295 as the regular in 1947, and a twenty-six-year-old chunky kid fresh from Triple-A St. Paul named Roy Campanella, and both of them needed the playing time more than Bragan.

That day, Dodgers president Branch Rickey came down to the field looking for Bragan. In the spring of 1947, the Alabama-born Bragan had been one of the players opposed to Rickey's plan to break baseball's color barrier with Jackie Robinson. But he had also been honest with Rickey in a meeting during spring training, earning the president's respect, and Bragan eventually accepted and then became friends with Robinson. But this time, Rickey didn't want to talk about race relations. He wanted to offer Bragan a new job: as player–manager of the Dodgers' Texas League club, the Fort Worth Cats. Bragan recalled Rickey's words years later: "Bobby, you're not playing. If you'd like to play, there's an opening in Fort Worth where you can be the catcher and the manager. Would you be interested?"

Bragan's response: "I can go right now." Years later, Bragan had an even better one-liner: "I knew it was the best thing to do," he said. "I had spent so much time on the bench since April, my teammates had begun calling me judge."

Rickey had fired Les Burge as the Cats' manager after the club lost 12 of 16 games, and relief pitcher George Dockins—with the help of former Dodgers manager Burt Shotton—had been running the club on an interim basis until a permanent replacement was named by the parent club. Although he had never managed before, Bragan took to the job as a player–manager. In his first game at the helm, the Cats, who had gone 11–0 under Dockins and Shotton, moved into first place, and they stayed there the rest of the season, even after losing hotshot pitching prospect Carl Erskine to the Dodgers at the end of July and suffering through an injury-plagued stretch in September.

Bragan also began to show his fiery side, one that would earn him a reputation as one of the game's greatest umpire-baiters. In a game in Shreveport in late July, in protest of what he perceived to be a bad call, he had relief pitcher Eddie Chandler stage a slow-down strike. Umpire Frenchy Arceneaux practically had to drag Chandler out of the bullpen. Then, after throwing his warm-up pitches to Bragan and having a brief conference with his manager, Chandler began to throw with third baseman Beans Marionetti. Arceneaux tossed the pitcher out of the game. Bragan, his point apparently made, stayed. "I didn't believe in cussing, ranting or raving, but I would stay up nights thinking how I could get to them," Bragan said years later. "And I came up with a few ideas.

At the end of the season, Fort Worth took playoff series from Shreveport and Tulsa to claim the pennant but lost to Birmingham in the Dixie Series. A record crowd of 17,121—the biggest since the Dizzy Dean–Ray Caldwell showdown in 1931—showed up for the first game at the Barons' Rickwood Field. Among them were Bragan's seven brothers.

The next season, Bragan's Cats won one hundred games but fell to Tulsa in the league championship series. Bragan managed Fort Worth into the playoffs in 1950 and 1952 but resigned after the 1952 season. He went on to manage Hollywood and Spokane in the Pacific Coast League and the Pittsburgh Pirates, Cleveland Indians, and Milwaukee–Atlanta Braves in the big leagues. Each winter, he returned to Fort Worth, which had become his home.

The expansion Montreal Expos hired him in 1969, but before the team could play a game, he was summoned home. The Texas League, reeling under the minors' prolonged slump of the late 1950s and 1960s, needed a new president. Bragan had already been instrumental in getting San Antonio back into the league for the 1968 season, working with local university and business leaders to replace the club that had left after the 1964 season. Still, he was taking over a league with serious problems, including attendance that had fallen from a postwar high of 2,041,043 to 609,890 in 1967.

In an attempt to boost interest, he helped organize the one-year Dixie Association, an experiment with the Southern League in which the leagues' fourteen teams played a combined schedule. In 1972, the Texas League survived the loss of Dallas–Fort Worth—which was drawing two-hundred-thousand-plus a year—to the major leagues, in part by expanding into new markets in Alexandria and Midland. A new wave of innovative team operators began to come into the league in the 1970s, including John Begzos in San Antonio, Jim Paul in El Paso, and Bill Valentine in Arkansas, and attendance began to climb.

After eight years in charge of the league, Bragan was named the president of the National Association of Professional Baseball Leagues in 1976. He modernized the governing body of the minor leagues, landing the organization a new office, setting up an annual trade show, and establishing an employment bureau in his three years in the job. After that he worked for the Texas Rangers and served as a goodwill ambassador for the game all over the world, besides starting up a foundation to award college scholarships. He also helped bring the Cats back to Fort Worth as a member of the independent Central League, and he took part in the rebuilding of Fort Worth's LaGrave Field.

In recognition of his years as a player, manager, and executive in the league, the Texas League voted in 2003 to name its championship trophy after him.

=26=
OPENING DAY, 1950

DICK BURNETT WAS A MAN WITH A FLAIR FOR THE DRAMATIC.
The native of the east Texas town of Gladewater had made and
lost and made another fortune in the oil business when in 1948 he
bought the Texas League's Dallas franchise for $550,000—report-
edly three times what the team was worth.

He spent $250,000 renovating the team's stadium, which he
immodestly renamed Burnett Field. He was investigated by the
commissioner's office for an incident in which he threw "a type-
writer or something" out a press box window. He was known to
rush to the backstop behind home plate and threaten to send players back to his farm club in Texarkana.

But "Rampant Richard" Burnett had big plans for Dallas, plans
that included luring a major-league team to the city. One part of
his plan was to win a series of pennants (he tried his best, but
Dallas' only championship came in 1953, a year in which the team
went on to win the Dixie Series). Another part was to drum up as
much baseball publicity as possible, which led to his most famous
promotion.

In 1950, as a way to break the Texas League record for opening-
day attendance (at the time, 16,018 in Fort Worth in 1930), he got
permission to play in the Cotton Bowl, which could hold more

than seventy-five thousand. To get people to show up, he wanted a lineup of former stars to put on Dallas Eagles uniforms and face one Tulsa hitter in the top of the first inning. Most of the old-timers Burnett contacted were cool to the idea, except for fifty-one-year-old Charlie Grimm, who was making the princely sum of $30,000 a year to manage Burnett's club. But when 63-year-old Ty Cobb agreed to come to Dallas, the others began to fall in line. Besides Grimm at first base and Cobb in center field, the Eagles would have Charlie Gehringer (46 years old at the time) at second base, Frank "Home Run" Baker (64) at third, Travis Jackson (46) at shortstop, Duffy Lewis (61) in left field, Tris Speaker (62) in right, and Mickey Cochrane (47) at catcher. The pitcher was Dizzy Dean, the youngest of the bunch at 40.

Publicity was widespread, in an era when most people in Dallas had never seen a big-league game, much less a lineup with three members who at the time were in the Baseball Hall of Fame (all but Grimm and Lewis would eventually be enshrined in Cooperstown). One Dallas bank bought 15,100 tickets for distribution to high school students. To encourage early arrivals, the first fan in each section received a ball autographed by the old-timers.

The players were honored with a pregame parade through downtown Dallas, and many in the crowd of 54,151 showed up early enough to watch them take batting practice (Cobb reportedly hit several balls into the stands, just to show he could still handle the bat). The Kilgore Rangerettes drill team performed on the field before the game, and Governor Allan Shivers, who at forty-two barely qualified as an old-timer himself, threw out the ceremonial first pitch. Dean walked the first Tulsa batter, Harry Donabedian, on a 3–2 pitch, and then the regular Dallas players took to the field. Dean got into an orchestrated rhubarb and was tossed from the game.

Of course, the attendance broke the Texas League record for

opening day. It still stands as the biggest crowd in league history and the second biggest in the history of the minor leagues.

The stunt was one of Burnett's biggest success stories, but he never was able to realize his plan to bring the majors to Dallas. While on a business trip to Shreveport in 1955, he died of a heart attack. He was fifty-seven.

=27=
BILL RUGGLES

IN GROUP PHOTOS TAKEN AT ANNUAL MEETINGS OF THE
Texas League's owners from the 1920s to the 1940s, there's always
a short, slightly chubby man in the frame, looking somewhat out
of place. The man was William Ruggles, and although he never
owned or operated a baseball team in his life and never played
beyond the sandlots of childhood, in many ways he was as important as any of the men in those group photos.

Born in Austin in 1891, Ruggles grew up loving baseball. He
was the sports editor at the *Houston Post* from 1910 to 1916 and
worked at the *Galveston News* for two years after that. After serving in World War I, he joined the *Dallas Morning News* in 1919.

But it was another job that earned him a place in the history of
the league. In 1920, he became the Texas League's official statistician and unofficial historian, and he set out to chronicle the circuit's earliest days. He contacted many of the veteran players,
including some who had been around for the founding of the
league in 1888, and in 1932 he published *The History of the Texas
League*, complete with rosters and year-by-year reports on the
league's business. Periodically, he produced and published league
record books, even as his career at the *Dallas Morning News* continued. He moved from sports editor to associate editor of the edi-

torial page in 1926 and, upon returning from World War II in 1943, was named editor of the editorial page.

In 1951, he produced an updated edition of *The History of the Texas League*, which included an all-time roster of players and umpires, brief histories of the league's cities, and summaries of each season. He also wrote profiles of some of the league's most notable figures, from John McCloskey to Branch Rickey to Paul LaGrave, and he included an extensive interview he conducted with McCloskey, the acknowledged father of the Texas League, in 1931.

For the sake of thoroughness, Ruggles included a brief biography of himself in the chapter on the league's presidents because he filled in for president J. Doak Roberts when Roberts fell ill and died in 1929. And while he mentions that he served in both wars and was the proud secretary of the Ex-Students Association at the University of Texas, he never mentioned two other brushes with fame: he coined the phrase "right to work" in an editorial in 1941—promoting workers' right to keep their jobs without joining a union—and he was well-known in the Dallas area for his light-hearted poetry.

Ruggles followed up his history of the league with another book, *Roster of the Texas League,* a compilation of biographical information on almost 6,300 players, managers, and umpires, in 1952. "It was a labor of love," he once said.

Bill O'Neal, who wrote an extensive history of the league in 1988, noted Ruggles's contribution: "His lifelong devotion to the Texas League . . . preserved an invaluable mine of materials about the first seven decades of the loop."

Ruggles retired from the *Morning News* in 1960, but he continued to be active in organizations ranging from the Texas Poetry Society to the Sons of the Republic of Texas. He died in 1988 at the age of ninety-seven.

=28=
REX BARNEY

THE FIRST PITCH REX BARNEY EVER THREW IN THE MAJOR
leagues hit batter Eddie Stanky square in the back. It was a sign of
things to come.

The Brooklyn Dodgers had signed the hard-throwing right-
hander right out of high school in Omaha, Nebraska, in 1943, and
by August of that year he was in the big leagues—hitting batters
and walking them at an alarming rate. In 45⅓ innings that season,
he walked forty-one. The Dodgers' Branch Rickey sent Barney to
the minors the next year, and he didn't return to the big leagues
until 1946. Even then, he struggled for two more seasons, averaging almost a walk—and almost a strikeout—an inning. Rickey
tried everything he could think of to improve Barney's control,
from sending him to a hypnotist to leaving him in Florida to work
one-on-one with a pitching coach after the rest of the team had
gone north. "Barney pitched as though the plate was high and outside," Bob Cooke wrote of him in the *New York Herald-Tribune*.

In 1948, Barney finally seemed to have his fastball under control. That season, he went 15–13 with a 3.10 earned run average,
striking out 138 and walking 122 in 246⅔ innings, with 4 shutouts and 12 complete games. He even threw a no-hitter, beating

the powerful New York Giants at the Polo Grounds on September 9—in the middle of a driving rainstorm.

Two weeks later, though, he broke his leg in two places while sliding into second base. He was never the same, as the delicate balance he had worked to achieve in 1948 disappeared. He went 9–8 in 1949 and was 2–1 in 1950 when Rickey sent him to the minors.

In May 1951, Barney was assigned to Fort Worth, the Dodgers' affiliate in the Texas League, to work with Cats manager and former big-league catcher Bobby Bragan. But nothing seemed to help there, either. In his first start with the Cats, Barney walked 16, tying a Texas League record. He faced 41 batters and was behind in the count to all but 7 of them. To make matters worse, he also had 2 wild pitches. Surprisingly, though, he left the game in the eighth inning down just 2–1. The Cats eventually lost to the Houston Buffs, 6–2.

"Barney, who exhibited a world of speed and a good, sharp-breaking curve, walked home just one run," the *Houston Post* reported. "And four times he pulled out of the hole with the bags loaded. He said after the game he was not discouraged, that he knew he was wild, but that he hoped plenty of hard work in the minors could cure him." Unfortunately, it didn't. Ten days later, he walked seven in 1⅔ innings in a 7–3 loss to Dallas.

Through all his troubles, Barney never lost his sense of humor, though. Before a game against Shreveport in May 1951, he was playing catch with thirteen-year-old batboy Marvin "Red" McIntyre, and the youngster overthrew Barney. The ball sailed into the Fort Worth dugout, sending teammates scattering. "That's all right, Red," Barney said. "I know just how you feel."

Barney was never able to overcome his wildness in the minors, and as a consequence he never made it back to the majors. But he found another career in baseball—from 1964 to 1997, he was the public address announcer at Baltimore Orioles games. He became well-known for his call of "give that fan a contract" whenever a spectator made a good catch in the stands, and he followed each announcement with a hearty "thank you." When Barney died on August 12, 1997, the Orioles played their game that night without a PA man in his honor.

=29=
BOB TURLEY

THE ST. LOUIS BROWNS KNEW THEY HAD A GOOD PROSPECT when they signed seventeen-year-old Bob Turley in 1948. The East St. Louis native threw hard—in the mid-nineties by all estimates. He was big for his era: 6 foot 2 and 205 pounds. He had the kind of stuff that could produce a no-hitter just about anytime he went to the mound. It was just a matter of time.

He went 9–3 for Belleville, Illinois, in the Illinois State League in 1948 and 25–5 for Aberdeen, Maryland, in the Northern League the next season. That led the Browns to assign him to Double-A San Antonio, where he was the Missions' opening-day pitcher in 1950. But after two seasons of overpowering hitters in the lower classifications, he struggled at Double-A and was sent back to Class A Wichita, where he went 11–14 but learned how to pitch. "Joe Schultz, who was the manager at Wichita, really helped me a lot," Turley said in the *Sporting News* in 1951. "In my first two years I was able to win because I threw the ball by hitters. But I learned I couldn't do that in the Texas League or at Wichita. Schultz taught me a lot about how to pitch, how to change up and improve my curveball."

The work paid off in 1951 when Turley came back to San Antonio. Missions veteran pitcher Homer Gibson helped show him how to hide the ball from hitters, and with that knowledge he got off to a 10–2 start.

The highlight of his season came on August 11 against Tulsa. The right-hander was going for his twentieth victory of the season that night at Mission Stadium, in front of a bigger-than-usual crowd of 3,143. San Antonio, which was coming off its first and only Dixie Series title, was headed for the postseason again. The Oilers were headed for a seventh-place finish.

San Antonio gave Turley a 2–0 lead in the fifth, and it looked like he was headed for another double-figures strikeout total and win number twenty. But in the eighth, Tulsa's John Temple led off with a single, and Jim Kirby followed with a sinking liner to center. Missions center fielder Bobby Balcena let the ball roll between his legs, and by the time it was retrieved, both runners had scored. The game went to extra innings.

Tulsa's Bob Curley was as tough to hit as Turley that night, not allowing a hit between the fifth and tenth innings. Turley continued to mow down the Oilers hitters, striking out two men each in the eighth, ninth, eleventh, and twelfth innings.

In the top of the sixteenth, Tulsa's Dewey Williams walked and was sacrificed to second. With two away, Kirby lofted what looked like a routine fly ball to right field. But Missions right fielder Omer Tolson dropped it, and Williams, who was running all the way, scored the go-ahead run. With two outs in the bottom of the sixteenth, it looked like Turley was going to get the loss, but Balcena hit a solo home run to left to make it 3–3. One out later, the game was called a tie because of the league's 11:50 P.M. curfew.

Turley wound up allowing 12 hits—all singles—and he walked 9. In sixteen innings, Turley struck out 22 Tulsa hitters in what still stands as a league record for strikeouts in a game. The marathon game also established a record for combined strikeouts in a game, 28, since Tulsa's Curley and Dave Jolly had 6 between them. But that record lasted less than three weeks. On September

3, Turley struck out 14, and league strikeout champion Wilmer "Vinegar Bend" Mizell of Houston had 17 in the Buffs' 3–2 victory over the Missions.

Turley finished the year with a record of 20–8 in 34 appearances, struck out 200 in 268 innings, and was named the Texas League Pitcher of the Year, even though he didn't lead the league in any statistical category.

Turley made one appearance in the major leagues in 1951, getting the loss for the Browns against the Chicago White Sox on September 29. He didn't make it to the big leagues to stay until 1954, when the Browns became the Baltimore Orioles. That season, he went to a no-windup delivery to cut down on his walks, and it helped him lead the league in strikeouts, with 185. He still led the league in walks with 181, but he was good enough to attract the attention of the New York Yankees, who landed him as part of an eighteen-player deal between the 1954 and 1955 seasons.

Turley's time to shine came with the Yankees, as he pitched in five World Series and won the Cy Young Award in 1958, going 21–7 with 168 strikeouts and just 128 walks.

Mike O'Connor was one of the pioneers of the Texas League, taking part in every season from 1888 to 1905. He batted .401 in 1896 but may be best known as the manager of the powerful Corsicana Oil City Oilers in 1902. *(Texas League photo)*

John McCloskey is considered the father of the Texas League because he organized efforts to get the league started in the winter of 1887-88. He went on to manage, play, and umpire in the league through the 1899 season, and he stayed in baseball in one form or another until 1930. *(University of Texas at San Antonio Institute of Texan Cultures)*

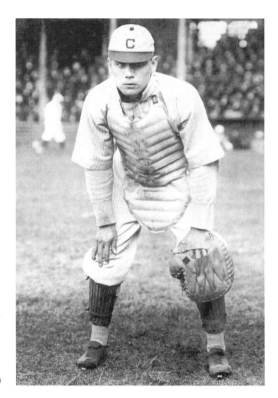

Jay Clarke was the catcher on one of the greatest teams in Texas League history, the 1902 Corsicana Oil City Oilers. Clarke is best known for his role in the team's 51–3 victory over Texarkana, a game in which he drove in a record 16 runs. *(The Sporting News photo)*

Harry Ables still holds the league record for strikeouts in a season, 310, set during his amazing 1910 season in San Antonio. Ables returned to the league as club president in the 1920s, pitching games in 1925 and 1926 as publicity stunts. *(University of Texas at San Antonio Institute of Texan Cultures)*

Clarence Kraft was one of the key players during the Fort Worth Cats' domination of the Texas League from 1919–25, leading the league in homers in 1922, 1923, and 1924. In the final games of his career, he led Fort Worth to a Dixie Series victory over Memphis. *(Photo courtesy of the Mark Presswood collection)*

Joe Pate teamed with Paul Wachtel and Lil Stoner to give the Fort Worth Cats the best pitching in the Texas League from 1919–25. *(Photo courtesy of the Mark Presswood Collection)*

SAN ANTONIO MISSIONS . . . 1950

Back row, left to right: Frank Mancuso, catcher; Procopio Herrera, pitcher; Eddie Albrecht, pitcher; Dr. William Cole, Trainer; Joe Lutz, infielder; Wes Hamner, infielder; Joe Frazier, outfielder; Walter Brown, pitcher.

Middle row, Jim Dych, outfielder; Frank Saucier, outfielder; Mel Held, pitcher; Rocco Ippolito, outfielder; Frank Biscan, pitcher; Johnny Sullivan, infielder; Louis Sleater, pitcher.

Front row, Hal Hudson, pitcher; John Gibson, pitcher; John Pavlick, pitcher; Don Heffner, Manager; Dan Baich, catcher; Andy Anderson, infielder; Charles Grant, infielder.

Batboys: Frank Castilla and Thomas Hatfield.

Ike Boone hit .402 for San Antonio in 1923—the last time anyone in the Texas League has topped .400. *(Photo courtesy Baseball Hall of Fame)*

OPPOSITE TOP: The 1950 **San Antonio Missions** won the city's only Dixie Series championship with a game 7 decision over Nashville. *(Texas League photo)* BELOW: The 1923 **Fort Worth Cats** were the only team from the Cats' run of Texas League pennants that did not win more than 100 games, but they still managed to run away with the title and beat New Orleans in the Dixie Series. *(Photo courtesy of Mark Presswood collection)*

The greatest manager in Texas League history, **Jake Atz** won six consecutive pennants and five of the first six Dixie Series while leading the Fort Worth Cats. He managed in the Texas League for 18 seasons. *(Photo courtesy of the Mark Presswood collection)*

Flamboyant **Dick Burnett** brought a new sense of excitement to Dallas when he bought the team in the 1940s. *(Photo © 2004 San Antonio Express-News; reprinted with permission)*

A 13-year Texas League veteran, spitball pitcher **Snipe Conley** was the victim of a prank by Wichita Falls that eventually led to the Spudders forfeiting a game to Dallas. (The Sporting News *photo*)

Gene Rye pulled off one of the greatest single-inning performances in Texas League history when he hit three home runs in Waco's 17-run eighth against Beaumont in 1930. (The Sporting News *photo*)

Dizzy Dean blazed through the Texas League in 1931, leading in wins (26), strikeouts (303), and complete games. The league's player of the year in 1931, Dean tried to make a comeback with Tulsa in 1940 following arm injuries. *(Photo courtesy Baseball Hall of Fame)*

Galveston's **Ed Cole** threw the first perfect game in Texas League history, beating Tulsa 1–0 on July 1, 1935, during his rookie season. Cole went on to pitch seven seasons in the Texas League, going 81–82. *(University of Texas at San Antonio Institute of Texan Cultures)*

Shreveport's **Dave Wilhelmi** had the only other perfect game in league history, beating Arkansas 2–0 on May 4, 1983. *(Texas League photo)*

Tulsa's **Marty Scott** played all nine positions during the 1981 Texas League All-Star Game. *(Photo courtesy Mark Presswood collection)*

Texas Rangers manager **Billy Martin** had a good time managing against the Texas League all-stars in 1974, inserting himself and most of his coaching staff into the game. *(Photo © 2004 San Antonio Express-News. Reprinted with permission)*

Tulsa slugger **Jim Beauchamp** ended the 1963 Texas League All-Star Game with a grand slam. *(Photo © 2004 San Antonio Express-News. Reprinted with permission)*

Future big-league umpire—and Arkansas Travelers general manager—**Bill Valentine** handles a dispute during the 1959 all-star game between players from the Texas League and the Mexican League. *(Texas League photo)*

Nicknamed "Prince" because of his Hawaiian heritage, **Hank Oana** was one of the more versatile players in Texas League history. He was a hard-hitting outfielder before World War II, but after the war he was converted to pitching—and led the league in wins with 24. *(Texas League photo)*

Shreveport player/ manager **Salty Parker** led his team to a 19-inning victory over Fort Worth in the 1942 playoffs—the longest postseason game in league history, and one of the last before the three-year hiatus for the war. *(Texas League photo)*

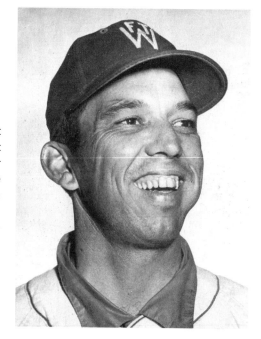

The Brooklyn Dodgers sent **Bobby Bragan** to Fort Worth as player/manager in 1948, and he led the team into the playoffs in 1948, '49, '50 and '52. Bragan later served as the president of the league, and the championship trophy is named after him. *(Photo © 2004 San Antonio Express-News. Reprinted with permission)*

Fort Worth Cats catcher **Bobby Bragan** chases Tulsa's **Mickey Rutner** back toward third base during a close contest at Fort Worth's LaGrave Field. *(Texas League photo)*

The starting outfield for the greatest old-timers team ever assembled: **Tris Speaker**, **Ty Cobb**, and **Duffy Lewis**, who came to the Cotton Bowl in Dallas for Dick Butler's opening day promotion in 1950. A league-record 54,151 saw the game, which included former all-stars at every position. *(Photo courtesy Baseball Hall of Fame)*

Dallas owner **Dick Burnett** (middle row, second from left) brought high ambitions to the league, including the 1950 opening-day promotion with a field full of old-timer all-stars. **William Ruggles** (back row, third from right) was the statistician and historian of the Texas League for many years, compiling at least three books on the league. *(Texas League photo)*

Fort Worth pitcher **Rex Barney** walked a league-record 16 batters on May 13, 1951. *(Photo © 2004* San Antonio Express-News. *Reprinted with permission)*

Wilmer Mizell was a hard-throwing left-handed pitcher for Houston in 1951. Following a long major-league career, Mizell was elected to Congress from North Carolina. *(Photo © 2004* San Antonio Express-News. *Reprinted with permission)*

Bob Turley, a hard-throwing 20-year-old, set the Texas League record for strikeouts in a game when he posted 22 in a 16-inning contest in 1951. *(Photo copyright 2004* San Antonio Express-News. *Reprinted with permission)*

San Antonio's **Bob Turley** jumped into prominence with his 22-strikeout performance in 1951, in this case earning attention from New York Yankees manager **Casey Stengel** (left) and another young prospect, **Billy Hunter** (right). *(Photo copyright 2004* San Antonio Express-News. *Reprinted with permission)*

Dave Hoskins opened the door for African American players in the Texas League when he signed with—and starred for—the Dallas Eagles in 1952. *(From the collection of the Texas/Dallas History and Archives Division, Dallas Public Library)*

Joe Pignatano unofficially hit two home runs in the same at-bat for the Fort Worth Cats. He went on to play in the big leagues for the Dodgers, Athletics, Giants, and the 1962 New York Mets. *(Photo courtesy Los Angeles Dodgers)*

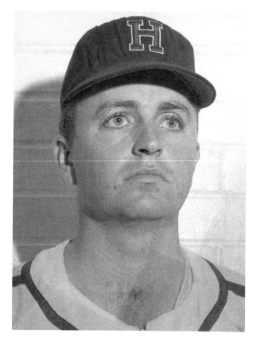

Billy Muffett pitched the first no-hitter in the Texas League playoffs, leading Shreveport past San Antonio in the clinching game of the 1955 post-season. *(Photo © 2004 San Antonio Express-News. Reprinted with permission)*

Ken Guettler shattered the Texas League record for home runs in 1956, hitting 62—a mark that still stands as the league standard. *(Texas League photo)*

Austin native **Charlie Gorin** led the Austin Senators to the Pan American Series title in 1959, pitching a no-hitter against Mexico City in the deciding game. *(Photo © 2004 San Antonio Express-News. Reprinted with permission)*

Austin Senators
PAN AMERICAN ASSOCIATION
CHAMPIONS 1959

Bottom row left to right: DICK LEE, BAT BOY; RICK HERRSCHER • CHUCK BUHELLER •
BILL THOMPSON • BOBBY HENDLEY • ERNIE CHRISTOFF • HOWIE BEDELL •
Second row - - - JACK CAFFERY • J.W. JONES • BILL SHIELDS • MIKE LUTZ •
ROSS CARTER • BOBBY KNOOP • TONY DIAZ •
Third row - - - GEORGE SHELL, business Mgr. • HAPPY MATHEWS, trainer •
PEPPER THOMAS • JIM CALLAWAY • CHARLIE GORIN • BILL HOLMES •
ERNIE WHITE, MANAGER • ALLEN RUSSELL, PRESIDENT •

The 1959 **Austin Senators** won the first Pan American Series, beating
the Mexico City Red Devils. *(Texas League photo)*

A young **Billy Williams** nearly gave up baseball after an unfortunate incident early in his first season with the San Antonio Missions. *(Photo © 2004* San Antonio Express-News. *Reprinted with permission)*

Dominican **Danilo Rivas** had two of the most impressive losses in Texas League history, striking out 18 in a game twice for the Rio Grande Valley Giants. *(*The Sporting News *photo)*

Lou Fitzgerald led the San Antonio Bullets to impressive seasons in both 1963 and '64, as the Houston Colt .45s affiliate made the playoffs both seasons and won the pennant in 1964. *(Texas League photo)*

BELOW: A skinny right-handed pitcher, **Chuck Hartenstein** showed remarkable durability in 1965 when he threw a number of extra-innings games, including an 18-inning effort on June 17, 1965. *(Texas League photo)*

One of the legendary tough guys in baseball, **Joe Medwick** was in the
stands when Arkansas and Memphis engaged in a memorable brawl at
Little Rock. *(Photo © 2004* San Antonio Express-News. *Reprinted with
permission)*

Jim Paul borrowed money to buy the El Paso Diablos and then used his marketing skills to fill the seats night after night at Dudley Field. *(Texas League photo)*

Former big-league umpire and Little Rock native **Bill Valentine** came up with dozens of novel ideas to promote the Travelers and make historic Ray Winder Field a popular spot in the summer. *(Texas League photo)*

Former no. 1 draft pick **Dave Righetti** set the Texas League record for strikeouts in a nine-inning game with 21 in 1978. He went on to be a star for the New York Yankees in the years after setting the Texas League record for strikeouts in a nine-inning game. *(Photo courtesy Mark Presswood collection)*

Mike Remlinger was a first-round draft pick in 1987, and he zoomed all the way to Double-A that year. In August, he just missed breaking a 72-year-old Texas League record when he struck out the first nine batters of the game. Mike Remlinger was a dominating pitcher for the Shreveport Captains in his first season as a pro. The San Francisco Giants' no. 1 draft pick struck out the first nine batters in a game in August. *(Texas League photo)*

DIABLOS   Mike Felder / Outfield

DIABLOS   Stan Levi / Outfield

Mike Felder had nine RBIs in El Paso's 35–21 victory over Beaumont. **Stan Levi** drove in seven runs and scored seven times in El Paso's 35-21 victory over Beaumont. *(Texas League photo)*

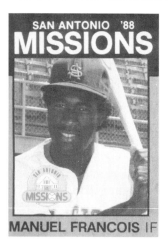

SAN ANTONIO '88

MISSIONS

MANUEL FRANCOIS IF

METS

BLAINE BEATTY   P

Manny Francois drove in the winning run in San Antonio's 1–0, 26-inning victory over the Jackson Mets in 1988. It was the longest game in Texas League history, and it took three days to complete. **Blaine Beatty** had a mixed day on July 16, 1988, as he took the loss in the resumption of a 25-inning scoreless game between Jackson and San Antonio, then got the victory in the regularly scheduled game that followed. *(Texas League photo)*

In 1997, Manager **Ron Roenicke** (left) and Pitching Coach **Guy Conti** led the San Antonio Missions to their first Texas League pennant since 1964. *(Texas League photo by Tom Kayser)*

Arkansas' **Tyrone Horne** hit for what is believed to be the only "homer cycle" in pro baseball history against San Antonio in 1998 when he connected on solo, two-run, three-run, and grand slam shots at Wolff Stadium. (Texas League photo)

Frank Howard had a memorable 1958 season with Victoria, hitting .356 in just 63 games with 27 home runs and 79 runs batted in. *(Texas League photo, courtesy Victoria College)*

El Paso's **Alex Cabrera** hit an amazing 31 home runs in the month of May and wound up with 35 homers and 82 runs batted in during 53 games for the Diablos. *(Texas League photo by Tom Kayser)*

San Antonio pitcher **Eric Gagne**'s combative nature made him the league's most dominant—and one of the most controversial—pitchers in 1999. Texas League pitcher of the year in 1999, he went on to set the major-league record for consecutive saves and won the National League Cy Young Award in 2003. *(Texas League photo)*

Roy Oswalt came up to Round Rock for on-start in 2001 and was so dominating he stayed the rest of the season. (Photo courtesy Mark Presswood collection)

Hank Greenberg led Beaumont to a 100-win season and a league championship in 1932. Greeberg led the league with 39 home runs, had 131 RBIs and was named the league's player of the year. He was one of 40 named in the initial class of the Texas League Hall of Fame in 2004. *(Texas League photo)*

One of the enduring power hitters in league history, **Russ Burns** led the league in RBIs four times in six seasons (1948–1953). Burns is second in home run production and RBIs in league history, and was elected to the Teaxs League Hall of Fame in 2004. *(Texas League photo)*

Keith Ginter learned of his promotion from Round Rock to the Houston Astros during the Express' celebration following the pennant-clinching game in 2001. *(Texas League photo)*

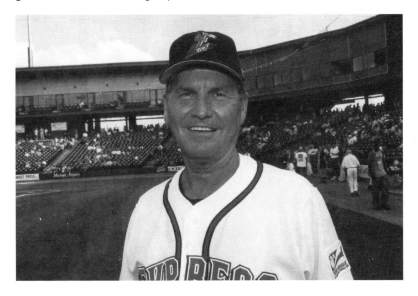

Former big-league manager **Jackie Moore** led the Round Rock Express to a Texas League title in the club's first season in the league. *(Texas League photo)*

Dudley Field, home of the El Paso Diablos until 1990, was the venue for the highest scoring game in league history when El Paso pounded Beaumont 35–21 on April 30, 1983. *(Texas League photo)*

=THIRD BASE=
STRUGGLE TO SURVIVE

=30=
DAVE HOSKINS

WHEN BRANCH RICKEY MADE THE DECISION TO BREAK BASE-
ball's color line in the 1940s, he conducted a scientific search, looking at dozens of players before choosing Jackie Robinson, who had the perfect blend of intelligence, temperament, and skill.

When Dick Burnett decided he was going to integrate the Texas League in 1952 he also conducted an exhaustive search—and then had to settle for what was available. Fortunately for the Dallas Eagles' owner, he got the league's equivalent of Jackie Robinson.

Dave Hoskins had broken a color barrier before, with Grand Rapids of the Central League, just a year after Robinson's debut with the Brooklyn Dodgers. He had been an outfielder when he did it, and he was knocked down regularly by opposing pitchers and thoroughly abused by opposing teams, as Robinson had been in 1947. He almost gave up, returning to the Negro Leagues and playing with the Homestead Grays before signing with the Cleveland Indians organization in 1950. The Indians sent him back to the Central League, this time to Dayton, Ohio, where once again he was a target for pitchers. Stretched out in a hospital bed after taking a pitch off his head, the former part-time pitcher decided he had had enough. "I was getting tired of having pitchers throw at me," he told the *Sporting News* later. "I made up my mind I would start throwing at other guys."

It helped that Hoskins spent the next winter barnstorming with Satchel Paige, who took one look at Hoskins's curveball and told him he was "wasting his time in the outfield." So Dave Hoskins became a full-time pitcher. He went 5–1 with Wilkes-Barre in the Eastern League in 1951, giving up 56 hits in 60 innings, with 35 strikeouts and 31 walks—okay numbers, but not exactly what Dick Burnett was looking for in his pioneer. The flamboyant Dallas owner—who like Rickey was integrating the league mostly out of conscience but partly with an eye on increased ticket sales—held tryout camps in north Texas during the winter and even signed a black player, second baseman Ray Neil, going into spring training.

Neil was a good fielder but a poor hitter, and Burnett needed a star, as Rickey had. After several meetings with officials from the Indians, who had a working agreement with the Eagles, Burnett agreed to take Hoskins—one of three African American players in the Cleveland farm system—as his man. He could not have made a better choice.

Hoskins won his first start, beating Tulsa 4–2—and getting a strikeout to end the game with the tying run at first—in front of a racially mixed crowd of 3,953 at Dallas's Burnett Field. And he kept right on winning—and filling ballparks. In Houston, 11,031 fans turned out to see him beat the Buffs 9–2. In Beaumont, a record crowd turned out—5,430, of whom 3,402 were black—to see him pitch. He filled parks in San Antonio and Fort Worth as well.

Attendance soared in Dallas, too, and Hoskins was accepted by his teammates, especially after his fast start. But there would be tough times, too. He took abuse from fans and opponents in some parks, and he could not stay in the same hotel with the team when it went on road trips.

BREAKING THE COLOR BARRIER

The second African American player in the Texas League was pitcher Bill Greason, who made his debut for Oklahoma City on July 31, 1952. Like Dallas' Dave Hoskins, Greason was not a baseball rookie—he had played in the Negro Leagues and was twenty-seven years old when he joined the Oklahoma City Indians. Greason was a hard thrower but was a bit on the wild side—he led the Texas League in walks in 1953, with 162. He appeared in three games for the St. Louis Cardinals in 1954, then played five more years in the minors, including two for Houston in the Texas League. After he retired in 1959, the pitcher known as "Boomer" became a minister.

Tulsa's first black player was Chuck Harmon, a two-sport star in baseball and basketball (he led the University of Toledo to the National Invitational Tournament [NIT] championship game in 1943). He had an auspicious start, hitting a home run on opening day in 1953. The next season, Harmon became the Cincinnati Reds' first African American player, and he wound up playing in 289 games in the majors.

San Antonio had two black players on its opening-day roster in 1953—catcher Charlie White and pitcher Harry Wilson. Wilson, a left-hander, had been in the St. Louis Browns organization since 1950. White was also signed by the Browns in 1950 after playing in the Negro Leagues. Both started the 1953 season well, but Wilson slumped at midyear and wound up 10–9 after starting out 9–4 while White hit .274 with 4 home runs and 46 RBIs. White played parts of two seasons in the majors with the Milwaukee Braves, but Wilson's career pretty much ended in 1953. He appeared in eighteen games for San Antonio in 1954 and just two for Wichita in 1955.

The player who broke the color barrier for the Fort Worth Cats in 1955 is the most famous member of the group: Maury Wills. The speedy shortstop struggled with Texas League pitching, hitting just .203, but he eventually made a big splash as a base stealer in the major leagues, swiping a record 104 for Los Angeles in 1962. ★

On June 9, Hoskins was scheduled to start in Shreveport. The Louisiana legislature had been considering a law that would have banned interracial sporting events, and the racial climate in Shreveport, just 190 miles east of Dallas, was significantly different from that in Texas. Hoskins received three letters the morning of the game. One said he would be shot if he sat in the dugout. The second said he would be shot if he went on the field. The third said he would be shot if he went on the mound. "I figured all three were from the same person," Hoskins told the *Sporting News* the next spring. "Probably just someone trying to scare me. I didn't tell Dutch Meyer, the manager of our club at the time, because I was afraid he wouldn't let me pitch. Dutch doesn't know about it to this day."

The only person he told was fellow pitcher Joe Kotrany, who sat in the bullpen and worried about him the entire game. Kotrany ran to the dugout before the ninth inning and asked his teammates to go out and surround Hoskins after the last out of the game. They did, and nothing happened—except that Hoskins got the win.

That kind of focus—Hoskins said later he had put the letters out of his mind by game time—and all the tips he learned from Paige and other Negro Leaguers helped him become the best pitcher in the Texas League in 1952. He led the league in wins (22), complete games (26), and innings pitched (280), and his ERA was an outstanding 2.12. He also hit .328.

The move worked for Burnett, too, as attendance in Dallas jumped from 228,263 to 266,532. Five other teams in the league saw their attendance rise as well.

Hoskins's arrival also spurred other teams in the league to integrate. Pitcher Bill Greason won his debut with Oklahoma City on July 31, and he and Hoskins pitched against each other on August 3 in front of Oklahoma City's biggest crowd of the season. In 1953, Tulsa and San Antonio added black players, with the Missions employing the first African American pitching battery, catcher Charlie White and pitcher Harry Wilson.

Hoskins went on to the major leagues, finishing 9–3 for the Indians in 1953 and appearing in fourteen games for the pennant-winning Indians the next season. But he hurt his arm in 1954 and spent the rest of his career in the minors, ending his career in 1959 with Dallas—which had moved up to the Triple-A American Association—and Spokane in the Pacific Coast League.

But for that one season, 1952, he had been the right man in the right place—the one Dick Burnett was looking for, even if he didn't know it at the time.

=31=
JOE PIGNATANO

AS HOME RUNS GO, THE ONE JOE PIGNATANO HIT FOR THE Fort Worth Cats against the Shreveport Sports on May 29, 1955, was fairly routine. The shot, at Shreveport's Texas League Park in the first game of a Sunday doubleheader, cleared the left-field wall by a good margin, but it was nothing unusual. Unless you count the fact that he had to hit it twice.

Pignatano was the Cats' catcher that season, his sixth in professional ball. As he had moved up in the Brooklyn Dodgers' farm system, his average had gone down, from a high of .375 in his rookie season to .248 in Elmira of the Eastern League in 1954. But he was a whiz behind the plate, and he eventually went to the big leagues, where he played in 307 games with the Dodgers, A's, Giants, and Mets and then worked as a major league coach for sixteen years.

He had a reputation as a smart player, but he made the most elementary of baseball mistakes in the first game of that May doubleheader in Shreveport when he stepped into the box against the Sports' Bill Moisan to start the second inning. He ripped a ball over the left-field wall, but it turned out that Cats shortstop Maury Wills was actually supposed to be up.

The Sports brought the gaffe to the attention of the umpires, and according to the rules Pignatano's homer was disallowed and

Wills was called out. Pignatano came up again in the proper spot in the order and worked Moisan to a 3–2 count. The Cats' catcher then hit a ball to almost exactly the same spot as he had moments earlier. This time it counted. The sequence was odd enough to merit substantial mention in both the Shreveport and Fort Worth newspapers the next day. But what made it even more unusual was the fact that it was one of just five homers Pignatano hit that season.

The catcher had one other moment of infamy. In the last at-bat of his career, he hit into a triple play. The game was the 120th and final loss of the season for the 1962 New York Mets.

=32=
BILLY MUFFETT

BILLY MUFFETT HAD THE SAN ANTONIO MISSIONS' NUMBER in the fall of 1955. In the last game of the regular season, the Shreveport Sports' twenty-four-year-old pitcher had stifled the Missions with a two-hit shutout, allowing just three base runners and wiping out two of them with double plays. That loss had knocked San Antonio out of first place in the league and set up a best-of-seven first-round series between the Missions and the third-place Sports.

A Fort Worth native, Muffett had been tough on the entire Texas League the second half of the season, going 10–4 after being called up from Class A Macon. But he had been toughest on the Missions. Even when they beat him in the first round of the playoffs, it wasn't entirely his fault—his teammates outhit the Sports but left thirteen men on base in a 4–0 loss.

The evenly matched teams went back and forth in their series, eventually reaching game six at Mission Stadium with the Sports holding a 3–2 edge. The pitchers were Muffett and San Antonio's Don Ferrarese, who had been 10–0 in the regular season, including a string of 38⅔ shutout innings.

The Sports were up 3–0 after three innings and added three in the fifth and four more in the sixth as Ferrarese was bombed for the second time in the series. San Antonio pitchers walked twelve, and the defense committed three errors as well. Muffett, on the other hand, was untouchable. He did not allow a base runner through the first five innings, then shook off a two-base error by shortstop Joe Koppe in the sixth to retire the side.

Muffett retired the last ten San Antonio batters in order and had the first no-hitter in Texas League playoff history. The closest play in the field had been a sinking liner by San Antonio third baseman Kal Segrist that Shreveport left fielder Leo Thomas snared with a running catch. He also battled with the game's final hitter, Joe Kirrene, a good curveball hitter. Muffett hung a curve to him, but he fouled it off. He fouled off four more pitches before finally grounding out to end the game and the series. "I thought he was going to stay up there all night," Muffett told the *San Antonio Light.*

Shreveport went on to win the Texas League pennant, beating Houston four games to three in the championship series. Muffett was the winning pitcher in game six, an 8–2 victory. But the Sports were swept by Southern Association champ Mobile in the Dixie Series, 4–0. Muffett lost his only start in that series.

Muffett signed with the St. Louis Cardinals organization during the off-season and went 28–16 in two more Texas League seasons with the Houston Buffs before getting his shot at the majors. He wound up playing parts of six seasons in the majors—and fourteen in the minors—before finding his calling as a coach in the bullpen. He was the St. Louis Cardinals' pitching coach for four years, including their championship season of 1967, then worked for the California Angels and the Detroit Tigers.

=33=
KEN GUETTLER

BY 1956, KEN GUETTLER HAD BEEN TRAPPED IN THE LOWEST levels of the minors for eleven years. At age twenty-nine, he wore thick, specially designed glasses when he played, and he could not fully straighten his right arm, the result of a childhood hockey injury. As a result, he was an unlikely looking player, one who probably didn't impress scouts all that much. But he finally caught a break—actually, a series of them—in 1956.

He may not have looked like a player, but he could hit. He won the triple crown while playing for Portsmouth, Virginia, in the Class B Piedmont League in 1952, hitting .334 with 28 homers and 104 runs batted in. In 1955, he hit a league-leading 41 homers for Portsmouth.

Guettler got his first break when the Piedmont League folded early in 1956. Frank Lawrence, who owned the Portsmouth team and had hired Guettler as a player–manager in 1955, recommended Guettler to a friend, Shreveport Sports owner Bonneau Peters. The Sports had Mike Lutz to play right field already, but Guettler got another break when Peters decided to take a chance on him. And he was fortunate again when Lutz showed up for spring training still lame from an ankle injury suffered in 1955. On top of everything else, Shreveport's Texas League Park had a short fence in left field, perfectly suited to the right-hander's strengths as a hitter.

Given all those breaks, Guettler responded with one of the biggest offensive outbursts in Texas League history.

He hit a home run against Houston on opening day. The second night of the season, he hit three off Buffs pitching, including one to send the game to extra innings. In the two games, he went 6 for 9 and drove in seven runs, prompting Houston manager Harry Walker—a former National League batting champion himself—to note that he was "one hell of a hitter."

The teams moved to Houston the next day, and after Guettler helped beat the Buffs with a two-run double in the first game at Busch Stadium, someone used underhanded means to stop him. When Guettler and the Sports arrived at the park for their next game, Guettler's specially made glasses were gone. There were no signs that anyone had broken in, leading the Sports to suggest that it was an inside job. "We are not accusing anybody, but circumstances certainly look a little strange," Shreveport manager Mel McGaha told the *Sporting News*. Walker and the Buffs denied any involvement, though—Walker was quoted later as saying "I don't know anything about it, but it was a great idea"—but because of the missing glasses, Guettler had to miss the game and the rest of the series while a new pair was shipped from the manufacturer.

The mysterious disappearance didn't slow him down for long. Guettler had 7 homers after the first two weeks of the season. In May, he went on a tear, hitting 18 in parks all over the league. He had another 3-homer night on May 28—each of them off a different Tulsa pitcher—and was a full month ahead of the pace set by Clarence "Big Boy" Kraft, who set the league record with 55 in 1924.

Guettler had just 6 homers in June, but he picked up the pace again in July, including a 2-homer, 5-RBI game against Tulsa on July 26. He went into August with 48, broke Kraft's record on

KEN GUETTLER'S NUMBER 63

According to Bill Valentine, one of the Texas League's other legends, Ken Guettler should have been credited with 63 home runs in 1956 instead of 62.

A future promotional innovator in the league, Valentine at the time was a twenty-four-year-old umpire in the Texas League. He was calling a game between Guettler's Shreveport Sports and the Fort Worth Cats at LaGrave Field when Guettler rocketed a ball off the upper level of advertising signs in left field. According to the ground rules, balls hitting that level were home runs, since the signs were set back from the outfield wall.

But third-base umpire Ken Burkhart—sixteen years Valentine's senior—ruled the ball was in play, and Guettler was credited with only a double. No amount of arguing from Sports manager Mel McGaha could change his mind, and Burkhart was so sure of the call he never asked any of his partners for help. "If he would have asked me, I'd have told him it hit the upper deck of signs," Valentine recalled years later. "He never did." ★

August 13, and reached 60 on August 26. He finished the season with a shot on September 2 that gave him 62.

His record-breaking season was part of a big year for home runs in the minors: Dick Stuart hit 66 for Wichita in the Western League, and four other leagues had homer champs who topped 50. For his season in the Texas League, Guettler was named the Rookie of the Year and Player of the Year.

But the next year he had run out of breaks. He hit a total of three home runs that season and was out of baseball by 1959, a victim of high expectations and limited patience.

He moved to Jacksonville, Florida, and went to work for the U.S. Postal Service. On Christmas Day, 1977, he died of a heart attack in his sleep at the age of fifty. His passing wasn't even noticed in the baseball community until March 1978, when the *Sporting News* ran an item about the sports editor of the *Shreveport*

Times finding Guettler's Rookie of the Year certificate while cleaning out a file cabinet. "It appears that Jack Fiser, then sports editor of the *Times*, filed it away with all good intentions of getting it to Guettler," *Times* sports editor Bill McIntyre told the *Sporting News*. "I'd like to get the scroll to Guettler after 22-odd years, but I know not of his whereabouts." Not long afterward, Guettler's sister, Selma Pett, contacted the magazine with the news of his death. "The Times has forwarded the rookie scroll to Mrs. Pett, who long has kept a scrapbook of her brother's baseball career," the *Sporting News* reported.

=34=
CHARLIE GORIN

CHARLIE GORIN HADN'T PITCHED PARTICULARLY WELL GOING into the critical fifth game of the inaugural Pan American Series on September 19, 1959. Gorin had been the losing pitcher for the Austin Senators in game two against the Mexico City Red Devils, outpitched by a thirty-nine-year-old former big-leaguer named Karl Drews. The 3–2 decision had been the only loss of the series so far for the Senators, the Texas League champions, who were taking on the Mexican League winners in hopes of reviving interest in both leagues.

A crowd of 2,338—a big turnout for the Texas League in the late 1950s, as attendance plummeted toward postwar lows—showed up for game five at Austin's Disch Field. In the audience at the little park in the bottomlands of the Colorado River just south of downtown were seven members of Gorin's family; he had grown up in Austin and had pitched in the College World Series for the Texas Longhorns. He also had been to the major leagues, though for just seven games for the Milwaukee Braves in 1954–55 and at thirty-one was clinging to hopes that he could make it back just once more. He would do all he could do to strengthen his case that Sunday afternoon.

A 5-foot-10, 165-pound left-hander who relied more on guile

and control than overwhelming stuff, Gorin retired the first twelve hitters to face him. In the top of the fifth, he went to a 3–1 count on the Devils' Marv Williams, and on the next pitch Williams hit a slow roller at Austin third baseman Pepper Thomas, who rushed the ball and misplayed it for an error. Williams advanced to second on a wild pitch. But Gorin struck out the next two hitters and got a popup from Roger Herrscher—to his brother Rick, who played outfield for Austin—to end the inning. Williams was the only hitter to reach a three-ball count for Mexico City.

Austin's light-hitting lineup had scored single unearned runs in the first and fourth against Drews for a 2–0 lead, but the Senators weren't having any more luck against the Mexico City hurler. Gorin continued to dominate. The Red Devils went down in order in the sixth, the seventh, and the eighth.

A standing ovation greeted Gorin in the top of the ninth. He got the number eight hitter in the order, then a pinch hitter, and then Red Devils leadoff man Ernesto Garcia hit a high fly to right. Bill Thompson squeezed it to end the first—and only—Texas League championship series decided by a no-hitter, and the only no-hitter of Gorin's professional career.

Austin manager Ernie White—as well as Gorin—said the veteran had pitched better that year, including an eleven-inning, 2–1 loss to Victoria. Gorin told the *Austin American* "I just had a lot of luck" in the no-hitter.

Gorin also talked about retiring after the game, mentioning that he had a wife and two children to support. But after Austin's management promoted the possibility of Gorin throwing back-to-back no-hitters all winter, he relented. He gave up a hit in the first inning of his first start of the 1960, and he wound up 8–8 for the year.

Gorin never made it back to the major leagues. But he did have some highlights during his career, especially game five of the 1959 Pan American Series.

=35=
BILLY WILLIAMS

IN 1959, SEVEN FULL YEARS AFTER DAVE HOSKINS BROKE THE color barrier, life was still tough for African American players in the Texas League. Ballparks had Jim Crow sections for black fans—in San Antonio's Mission Stadium, for example, it was far down the right-field line—and many major-league organizations had unwritten rules about how many black players they would carry. There was still one major-league team that had not integrated its roster: the Boston Red Sox, who finally added Pumpsie Green to their roster in April. Players had to endure racial taunts from opponents and fans. And there were other indignities as well, especially in the small towns where the Texas League had gone when Dallas, Fort Worth, and Houston bolted for Triple-A after the 1958 season.

The San Antonio Missions, in their first year of affiliation with the Chicago Cubs, had two African American players in 1959: J. C. Hartman, who had inherited the shortstop job for the Kansas City Monarchs when the Cubs had signed Ernie Banks, and a skinny kid from Alabama named Billy Williams.

Signed by the Missions off the Negro League club in Mobile, Alabama, Williams was just nineteen when he came to San Antonio. Hartman, who was twenty-four, was his roommate, at home and on the road.

Williams's talent was obvious—he could hit the ball, and hit it hard. After watching Williams use his long arms and powerful wrists to drive the ball all over the field at Mission Stadium one day, roving Cubs coach Rogers Hornsby sent a simple message to the front office: "Get that kid Williams up there as fast as you can. He's wasting his time here."

However, the Cubs kept Williams at San Antonio for a while as they converted him from first base to the outfield. He began working with Missions manager Grady Hatton and Hartman before games, fielding flies and learning how to play the new position. "Billy was so bad in he outfield that at first they made him wear a hard hat," Hartman said. "But they had a surplus of first basemen, so they made him an outfielder—and the rest is history."

There was still one more detour in Williams's path to the big leagues, and it started along the Texas coast. "I think it was the worst in Corpus Christi," Williams said years later. "We wanted to eat in the restaurant, but they said the only way we could eat was if we came in the back door and sat in the kitchen, next to the hot stove. It was hot, but I was hungry.

"The hardest thing we had to do by far was when the other guys would get off the bus to eat, and we had to wait for them to bring us some food."

Hartman and Williams were always the last ones off the bus— they had to stay in different hotels than the rest of the team—and they were the first ones picked up on the way to the ballpark each day.

Williams reached his breaking point when he and Hartman were not allowed to eat in a café in Victoria. Hatton had to plead with the owner to make the two players a meal, and then they had to eat in the kitchen. "Billy was really mad about that, and he said he was going home," Hartman said. Hartman drove Williams to the train station when they got back to San Antonio, and the young outfielder-in-the-making caught a train home to Mobile.

"That next day was a sad one at the ballpark," Williams said. "Grady Hatton didn't see me come in the next day with Jay [Hartman], and we always came in together. He asked Jay where I was, and Jay was talking real sad, and he said 'you can find him in Mobile.'"

The Cubs called Williams at home, asking him to come back. He said no. Owner Philip K. Wrigley called. No luck. Finally, the team sent Buck O'Neil, the former Monarchs manager, who was one of the first black scouts to work for a big-league team. "Buck O'Neil took me to the park in town, where I could see some of the friends I had grown up with," Williams said. "We started talking about what I was doing—and what they were doing—and [I] saw things a little differently. I realized I had a pretty good deal going on." Williams relented.

He rejoined the Missions for a series, and then the Cubs sent him to Triple-A, where he hit .670 the first week. He played in eighteen games for Chicago in 1959 and twelve more in 1960. In 1961, he was voted the National League Rookie of the Year.

Sometimes overshadowed by teammates Ferguson Jenkins, Ron Santo, and Banks, Williams quietly played in 1,117 consecutive games from 1963 to 1970, and for thirteen straight seasons he hit more than 20 homers and drove in at least 84 runs a year. He won a batting title in 1972 and finished second to Johnny Bench in voting for the National League's Most Valuable Player Award.

In 1987, in his sixth year of eligibility, Williams was elected to the Baseball Hall of Fame.

=36=
DANILO RIVAS

IN THE HISTORY OF BASEBALL NOT ALL PLAYERS RISE TO THE heights of the game, advancing all the way to the Baseball Hall of Fame. Some, like Texas League star Clarence "Big Boy" Kraft, had their shining moments in the minor leagues. And some, like pitcher Danilo Rivas, achieved their greatest glory outside the United States.

Rivas was a hard-throwing left-hander from the Dominican Republic who signed with legendary San Francisco Giants scout Chick Genovese in the late 1950s. He mowed down the batters in the Sophomore League in 1958, going 12–4 for Artesia, New Mexico, the Giants' Class D affiliate. In 1960, he was 15–5 with 222 strikeouts for Fresno in the Class A California League. The next spring, he was promoted all the way to Triple-A Tacoma. But after a 1–2 start, he was farmed out to the Victoria Giants of the Texas League. (In a time when the minors were suffering through tough financial times, the Giants had started the season in the Rio Grande Valley but moved to Victoria on June 10, replacing a team that had fled Victoria for Ardmore, Oklahoma, on May 27.)

Rivas was scheduled to make his second start of the season for Victoria on June 21, but the game was threatened because the rain-swollen Guadalupe River, which was adjacent to Victoria's

Riverside Park, was rising quickly. With finances tight, though, Victoria general manager Elmo Estes wanted to get the game in against the San Antonio Missions. So with the river lapping against some of the fences, Rivas went to the mound. He struck out two Missions hitters in the first. He struck out two more in the second. He struck out the side in the fourth and had two more every inning until the tenth. Three hitters—Daryl Robertson, Nelson Mathews, and Don Davis—whiffed three times each.

Victoria took a 3–0 lead into the fourth inning, but San Antonio tied it on a bases-loaded wild pitch that allowed in one run and a single that scored two more unearned runs. The Giants were unable to put up any more runs against San Antonio reliever Ron Goerger, and the game went to extra innings. In the top of the tenth, Rivas got his eighteenth strikeout of the night, but the Missions scored a run on a walk, an infield single, and a double, and wound up winning 4–3, not long before flood waters crept over the field.

Nearly two months later, Rivas was inserted into a game against Tulsa in the top of the ninth inning after Victoria reliever Tommy Bowers had given up a go-ahead homer and a single. Rivas got a fly ball and two strikeouts to end the inning. Victoria's Larry "Moose" Stubing homered in the bottom of the inning to tie the game at 7–7. Rivas wound up pitching eight more innings, matching his performance of June 21 by striking out eighteen hitters. He did not allow a hit until the fifteenth inning. But once again, the Giants' offense sputtered and the defense cracked. In the seventeenth, Tulsa's Jerry Marx led off with a blooper that got past Giants left fielder, Johnny Weekly—who tried to make a diving catch—for a double. Marx went to third on a groundout and scored when Johnny Lewis rolled a single to right field.

So in two outstanding performances—with thirty-six strikeouts in nineteen innings—Rivas got two losses. For the season, he went 9–8 with a 3.20 ERA for Victoria, which finished fifth in the six-team league. He went on to pitch until 1974, with teams from the Pacific Coast League to the International League to the Mexican League. He ranks among the leaders in career victories in Mexico after spending parts of seven seasons there.

But Rivas's greatest days weren't those two amazing performances in the Texas League, or his long career in Mexico. In 1969, pitching for the Leones de Escogido in the Dominican winter league, he threw fourteen innings without allowing a run in the league championship series, including a 3–0 shutout on two days' rest, earning him mention as the tournament's most valuable player. It was Rivas's second Dominican championship—he teamed with future Hall of Famer Juan Marichal to lead the Leones to the title in 1961 as well, winning a league-record thirteen games that season.

In fact, Rivas's career in the winter league fills the record book. He leads the Leones, whose history dates to the 1930s, in wins (75), starts (89), appearances (175), innings pitched (717) and, not surprisingly, strikeouts (469). He trails only Marichal in complete games (32 to 30) and is third in team history in shutouts, with 6.

Rivas retired to the Dominican Republic, where he remains a hero in the baseball-loving island nation. He was among the first people chosen to carry the torch that eventually would light the cauldron at the 2003 Pan American Games, which were hosted by the Dominican Republic.

=37=
LARRY MAXIE

THE SUMMER OF 1961 BELONGED TO LARRY MAXIE. SIGNED by the Milwaukee Braves in the spring of 1958 at the age of seventeen, he had risen through the Braves' farm system quickly, going from Class C Eau Claire to Double A Austin in three seasons.

A master of the breaking ball, Maxie had been promoted to the Senators late in the 1960 season but had gone winless in three decisions. In 1961, he started the season with Austin and won his first seven decisions in a row, the seventh a no-hitter against the Victoria Giants on June 14.

Maxie struck out seven and had just three close calls in the gem against the Giants. In the sixth, Victoria's Jerry Robinson hit a blooper into right field that second baseman Bill Lucas chased down for an out. In the eighth, the Giants' Dick Pawlow was thrown out on a close play at first after hitting a tapper up the first-base line. In the ninth, with Austin leading 2–0, Maxie walked the leadoff man, got a popup for the first out, then walked the next hitter. Senators manager Bill Adair sent reliever Phil Niekro to the bullpen to warm up, then walked to the mound. He motioned for a change, but it turned out to be for defense. The next batter bunted over the runners, but Maxie then got a popup to end the game.

A month later, Austin was on the losing end of a no-hitter, falling 11–0 to veteran Ramon Ramos at Poza Rica in one of the Pan American Association games between Texas League and Mexican League clubs. Ramos, who pitched sixteen years in the Mexican League, allowed just four base runners: two walks, a hit-batsman, and an error. It was the fourth of his career, but the first in the Mexican League since 1955.

Maxie pitched the next night in the Mexican city on the Gulf of Mexico. By then, he was 9–4 and had been chosen for the Texas League all-star team, which was due to play the Mexican League stars the next night in Mexico City. In front of a crowd estimated at five thousand, Maxie wasn't at his best at the start—he walked six and hit a batter. But Poza Rica's hitters couldn't touch his curveball. Austin scored a run in the first and three in the second to give him a lead, and he got tougher as he went along. He even overcame two infield errors by the Senators and wound up pitching his second no-hitter of the season—and second in thirty-one days—as Austin won, 5–0.

The games remain the only back-to-back no-hitters in Texas League history, and Maxie is the only pitcher in league history to throw two nine-inning no-hitters on one season. (The other is Bud Smith of Arkansas, who did it in two seven-inning games in 2000.)

Maxie finished his superb 1961 season 17–7 with a league-best ERA of 2.08 and was named the Texas League Pitcher of the Year. But his career didn't take off. He was just 2–3 with a 5.95 ERA in Triple-A in 1962, and he spent the next seven seasons in Triple-A in the Braves' farm system.

Maxie finally got his shot at the majors at the end of the 1969 season. But his big-league career consisted of just two games for the Atlanta Braves. He retired after the 1972 season.

=38=
JERRY HUMMITZSCH

JERRY HUMMITZSCH HAD FINALLY STARTED TO PULL THINGS
together in the spring of 1964. The right-handed pitcher, signed
to a $30,000 bonus by the Milwaukee Braves, had struggled his
first three years as a pro. He had quickly discovered that he couldn't
simply overpower minor-league hitters with the same fastballs
that had made him an All-American at Pueblo Junior College in
Colorado in 1961.

Hummitzsch had gone 9–10 at Boise in the Pioneer League in
1962, and he was 10–9 with the Austin Senators the next year,
showing promise (a seven-inning no-hitter against Tulsa in June
and a 3.13 earned run average for the season) and a good dose of
rawness as well (122 hits and 67 walks in 144 innings). But he
started the 1964 season strong, thanks in part to working out with
the Braves' big-leaguers in spring training. A hometown favorite for
Braves fans—he was from Sheboygan, Wisconsin—Hummitzsch
was 2–2 in his first four starts for Austin, striking out 23 in twenty-
seven innings with a 1.67 ERA.

On the night of May 21, Hummitzsch threw a three-hit, ten-
inning shutout to beat Fort Worth and even scored the winning
run in the bottom of the tenth. Jim Fanning, a special-assignments
scout for the Braves, was in the stands that night, and he told the

THE FIRST ACTIVE PLAYER TO DIE

Hummitzsch was one of at least five Texas-Leaguers who died during their careers. The first was the third baseman for the 1890 Waco club, William Stockcamp, who played under the name William Mussey. A one-paragraph item in the Waco newspaper noted that he "would be alive to-day, so the doctor say, if he had been taken to a hospital and nursed properly." Waco, at the time a city of twenty-five thousand, did not have a hospital. "It is sad indeed to know that a fond wife and help-less children mourn to-day simply because Waco has failed to do what other cities have done." ★

Austin American that the game was better pitched than the no-hitter from the year before. "It was a different type of game," Fanning said. "He was more of a pitcher. He was in compete command of the game all the way. He was never in trouble." Fanning said Hummitzsch was showing signs of becoming a big-league-caliber pitcher. "He could have won a game in the big leagues, for any team," he said.

After the game, Hummitzsch was relaxing on a training table in the Austin clubhouse, wearing an old straw hat. He asked Senators trainer Sam Ayoub where he could rent some fishing gear, since he had recently bought a boat from a former teammate, Bubba Wagner of San Antonio. Hummitzsch told Ayoub he and Wagner had big plans, as the pitcher was going to move to San Antonio during the off-season and join Wagner in a beer distrib-utorship. But on that Thursday night, he just wanted to jump in his new convertible and take teammate Walt Hriniak out for a short fishing trip.

They may or may not have gone fishing, but in any case they were out late. Sometime after midnight, on a winding road in the hills west of Austin, Hummitzsch lost control of the car he had bought with his bonus money. It tore through four guard posts and rolled over, tossing Hriniak clear but pinning Hummitzsch underneath. Hriniak survived, bruised and battered, and he went on to a short career in the majors and a long one as a hitting coach for the Boston Red Sox and Chicago White Sox and as a personal coach to stars like Wade Boggs and Frank Thomas. Hummitzsch died at the scene.

"What a future that kid had. Fantastic," Fanning told the *American*. "We're going out and looking for pitchers, and in our organization, Jerry was right at the top of the list. How close he was to the big leagues."

Several big-leaguers attended his funeral. Pallbearers included Braves pitchers Warren Spahn, Tony Cloninger, and Dick Kelley and catchers Joe Torre and Phil Roof. Team president John McHale and manager Bobby Bragan were at the service as well.

=39=
THE BULLETS

EARLY IN THE 1964 SEASON, A FAN CORNERED SAN ANTONIO
Bullets manager Lou Fitzgerald as he walked through the stands, complaining about the club's second baseman, a 5-foot-7, twenty-year-old kid who was in just his second season in professional baseball. The player in question had struggled at the plate the first week, not getting a hit.

"The way the clubhouse was at Mission Stadium, you had to walk through the crowd to get to the dugout," Fitzgerald recalled. "Well, you know [the player] got off to that bad start, and this guy comes up to me in the stands and says 'Lou, you're never going to win a pennant like we did last year with that little black kid at second base.'" The easygoing Fitzgerald just smiled and said he would check with Paul Richards, general manager of the parent Houston Colt .45s, about getting a replacement. That night, the Bullets' second baseman hit two home runs into the wind and stole three bases. "I saw that guy the next day and I said 'Well, I got ahold of Paul and he's sending us another second baseman,'" Fitzgerald said. "And the guy looks at me and said 'Oh no! He'll be just fine.'"

The Bullets' second baseman that season was Joe Morgan. He went on to hit .323, with 8 triples, 12 home runs, 90 runs batted in, and a league-high 42 doubles. At the end of the season, he was named the league's MVP and was on his way to a Hall of Fame career.

But Morgan wasn't the only star on what was one of the best teams San Antonio has ever fielded. His double-play partner, Sonny Jackson, was a sure-handed shortstop with as strong a work ethic as Morgan's. Almost every day of the season, they showed up early at the ballpark to take infield practice and work on turning double plays, often taking a hundred ground balls a session. The work paid off—San Antonio led the league in double plays in 1964, with 150.

In fact, the Bullets led the league in a lot of categories. Chuck Harrison, a hard-hitting first baseman from Abilene, led the league in home runs with 40 and in total bases with 297, and he was second in RBIs with 119. Jackson, as fleet afoot as Morgan, led the league in singles with 135. Right-hander Chris Zachary led the league in winning percentage, going 16–6, and tied for the lead in complete games with 16.

The Bullets had been good enough in 1963 to win the regular-season title—thanks in part to players like Jim Wynn and Jerry Grote, both of whom went on to play in the majors—but had lost to Tulsa in the championship series. The 1964 team had a combination of returning players like catcher Dave Adlesh and Harrison, minor-league veterans like relief pitcher Don Bradey and Clint Courtney (a character from the backwoods of Louisiana who served as Fitzgerald's coach and the team's backup catcher), and a core of good young players that included Morgan, Jackson, and pitcher Darrell "Bucky" Brandon.

Bradey played a critical role on the team. Richards had signed the thirty-year-old specifically to come into the game following young pitchers like Zachary and Brandon and preserve leads so they could win games and build confidence. It worked. Besides Zachary's 16 victories, Brandon went 15–7, and John Harms was

8–2. Bradey, dubbed the team's "relief ace," was 12–5 with a 2.81 ERA.

Like Morgan, the Bullets started the season slowly, trailing Tulsa through the first two months of the season. But in mid-June, San Antonio got hot, and on July 4 the Bullets moved into first place to stay.

But while the Bullets were taking control of the Texas League race, bad news was appearing in the local newspapers. In early August, the *Express-News* reported that the Colts were looking to sell the team and Mission Stadium. Five days later, Richards confirmed the move, citing poor attendance—the Bullets were averaging just 1,070 fans a game at that point—despite a first-place team. He also blamed annual financial losses of between $100,000 and $150,000 as well as poor coverage in the city's three newspapers. "It burns us up to see the Bullets buried on the back pages of the papers," Richards told the *Sporting News*. "We would prefer to move to a city where we would be the dominant sports attraction in town and where we would receive better play from the papers."

In retrospect, the Colts probably deserved some of the blame as well. The radio station that carried Bullets games—which was owned by the Colts' co-owner, Roy Hofheinz—was also the Colts' affiliate in San Antonio, and it broadcast Bullets games only when the Colts were not playing. Tickets for games at Colt Stadium in Houston were readily available in San Antonio— through the Bullets. And plummeting attendance throughout the minor leagues, a trend that began in the 1950s, was also a factor.

Still, the team continued to play well down the stretch and clinched its second consecutive regular-season title with a week left. San Antonio beat El Paso three games to one in the first round of the playoffs, setting up a rematch with Tulsa in the best-of-five championship series.

The Bullets won the first game 1–0 in sixteen innings, with

Jackson driving in the winning run on a sacrifice fly. Bradey pitched nine innings in relief and got the win. The next night, in what turned out to be the last professional game ever played at Mission Stadium, Tulsa evened the series with a 5–3 victory. But San Antonio won the next game in Tulsa, with Brandon giving up just two hits and two runs, and the Bullets clinched the pennant the next night behind Morgan's two doubles and Harrison's two hits and three RBIs.

The contest would be the last Texas League game for San Antonio for three years, as the Colts followed through on their threat and moved the team to Amarillo during the off-season (Amarillo drew 80,608 fans in 1965, compared with 85,808 in San Antonio in 1964). Mission Stadium, which had been built in 1947, was never used for baseball again. When a group spurred by Texas League president Bobby Bragan began to work on bringing a club back to the city in 1967, Houston's big-league team—which had become the Astros in 1965—refused to lease Mission Stadium. The Astros sold many of the old stadium's fixtures to the San Antonio Sports Association, which refurbished V. J. Keefe Field on the campus of St. Mary's University for the new team, but Mission Stadium sat empty and deteriorating until it was torn down in 1974.

The Texas League returned to San Antonio in 1968, but it took almost thirty years for another pennant winner to come to the city.

=40=
CHUCK HARTENSTEIN

IN SEVENTEEN SEASONS OF BASEBALL, CHUCK HARTENSTEIN had never pitched more than 11 innings in a game and rarely more than 9. But in the span of two months in the summer of 1965, the 5-foot-11, 165-pound right-hander from Seguin and the University of Texas pitched 12 innings in one contest for the Dallas–Fort Worth Spurs, 11 in another, and an amazing 18 in a third.

That 18-inning performance against the Austin Braves wasn't a league record—Harry Ables and Art Loudell both threw 23 in an epic showdown in 1910—but when combined with seven innings of relief by teammate Dick Burwell, it is a record for the longest performance by two pitchers in a game.

The 25-inning epic, finally won by Austin by a score of 2–1 well after midnight on June 18, made the record books. Besides the dual record by Hartenstein and Burwell, it also featured 7 innings of perfect relief—the first 7 of 11 thrown by Braves pitcher Cecil Upshaw. Dallas–Fort Worth first baseman John Boccabella had a record 32 putouts, and Spurs second baseman Charlie Benson recorded 14 assists.

Hartenstein lowered his earned run average from 2.72 to 2.32 in the game, giving up 1 earned run on 8 hits. He struck out 4 and walked 7. Fortunately, Hartenstein got through many of the innings easily, throwing just 189 pitches.

DALLAS–FORT WORTH'S ONE-RUN GAMES

Austin's 2–1 victory over Dallas–Fort Worth in twenty-five innings was the eighth of nine straight one-run games for the Spurs in June 1965, all played at Turnpike Stadium in Arlington, Texas. The Spurs were 5–4 in the contests, which included two doubleheaders and games against El Paso, Austin, and Amarillo. The last three games of the streak went to extra innings—an eight-inning game in the second game of a double-header scheduled for seven innings, the 25-inning epic and a 13-inning game. Dallas–Fort Worth finally ended the streak with a 5–2 victory over Amarillo on June 19.

The streak:

June 12	El Paso	6	Dallas–Fort Worth	5
June 13	El Paso	3	Dallas–Fort Worth	2
	Dallas–Fort Worth	3	El Paso	2
June 14	Dallas–Fort Worth	7	El Paso	6
June 15	Austin	1	Dallas–Fort Worth	0
June 16	Dallas–Fort Worth	3	Austin	2
	Dallas–Fort Worth	3	Austin	2
	(8 innings in scheduled 7-inning game)			
June 17	Austin	2	Dallas–Fort Worth	1
	(25 innings)			
June 18	Dallas–Fort Worth	2	Amarillo	1
	(13 innings)			

But he almost came out of the game early. Austin's Lee Tate, who had missed a number of games in 1965 after being hit in the head by another Dallas–Fort Worth pitcher, took offense at an inside pitch from Hartenstein in the fifth. When Tate's slow roller to first forced Hartenstein to hustle over to cover the base, Tate ran over him. Hartenstein landed on his left shoulder, suffering what he thought was just a bruise. He revealed many years later that the shoulder—of his nonpitching arm—was in fact separated on the play. But he went on throwing through the eighteenth before Spurs manager Whitey Lockman finally talked him into calling it a night. Austin scored the winning run on a single, a wild pitch, a sacrifice, and another single in the top of the twenty-fifth. Dallas–Fort Worth had a runner on third in the bottom of the inning but was unable to score.

The twenty-five-inning contest stood as a Texas League record until 1988, when San Antonio and Jackson battled for twenty-six innings.

Hartenstein suffered no ill effects from the game, going on to post the league's lowest ERA, 2.18, and a record of 12–7 for the Spurs. He made his big-league debut for the Chicago Cubs on September 11, 1966, and bounced back and forth between the majors and Triple-A until 1977.

=41=
PAT HOUSE

PAT HOUSE PITCHED WELL FOR THE AUSTIN BRAVES IN 1966. The twenty-five-year-old native of Idaho wound up leading the Texas League in ERA (2.13) and got ten of the team's sixty-seven wins that year. But it was an early-season game in El Paso that turned out to be his most noteworthy appearance of the season— and for an unlikely reason. On April 27, House drove in eight runs in the Braves' 19–4 romp over the Sun Kings. "I don't know what happened, really," he told the *Sporting News* after the game. "Every time I got up there, we had a guy on third base. You can't help but drive in some runs that way."

There aren't any official records on the subject, but the total is probably the biggest for a pitcher in league history, and it's a mark that likely won't be matched anytime soon, not in an era where few pitchers even come to the plate anymore because of the designated-hitter rule.

In his first at-bat in the top of the second, House doubled in two runs. In the third, he singled to drive in another. In the fourth, he drove in a run on a groundout. He came up again in the fifth and did the same. In the sixth, he doubled in two more. Walt Hrniak tripled to lead off the ninth, and House followed with a groundout to deep second to score a run and top off the eight-RBI day. He retired the side in the bottom of the inning for his second victory of the season. He gave up ten hits and four earned runs, with nine strikeouts and just one walk. "Everything good was happening to me," he told the *Sporting News*. "Even when I made an out, I got an RBI."

House went from Atlanta's organization to Houston's during the off-season, and he got to make his big-league debut in September 1967. In six games, he was 1−0 with a 4.50 ERA that year. He appeared in just eighteen games the rest of his major-league career, which lasted through the end of the 1968 season. In his entire time in the majors, he did not bat once.

=42=
JOE MEDWICK

AUGUST 29, 1968, WAS JOE "DUCKY" MEDWICK'S KIND OF night. Elected to the Baseball Hall of Fame earlier in the year, Medwick was in the stands at Ray Winder Field in Little Rock. The fifty-eight-year-old former outfielder was scouting the Cardinals' affiliate in the Texas League in his capacity as hitting coach for St. Louis.

Medwick had broken into the big leagues in 1932, joining the St. Louis Cardinals' freewheeling Gas House Gang. The feisty kid from New Jersey had fit right in with the likes of Leo Durocher, Frankie Frisch, Pepper Martin, and Dizzy Dean. With Medwick in the outfield, the Cardinals challenged for the National League pennant every year and won it in 1934.

Medwick was involved in one of the more famous incidents in World Series history that year, as he and Detroit's Marv Owen battled after a close play at third base in game seven. Both stayed in the game, but the Tigers' fans pelted Medwick with debris when he went to his position in left field. The barrage continued until the game had to be stopped and Medwick was replaced in the lineup.

Almost thirty-four years later, Medwick was a witness to—and almost a part of—one of the wildest incidents in Texas League history.

The Arkansas Travelers needed just one more win to clinch a playoff berth, and they were well on their way after John Sipin hit home runs in his first two at-bats against the Memphis Blues' Billy Hepler to give the Travelers a 6–2 lead. The third time Sipin came to the plate, Hepler threw a high, hard pitch that Sipin dodged, with the ball hitting him on the arm instead of the helmet. Players from both teams rushed onto the field, but they returned to the dugouts without incident, and the bottom of the fifth continued.

However, after two outs in the top of the sixth, Arkansas' Phil Knuckles fired one high and inside to the Blues' Greg Goosen, grazing him just under the bill of his helmet. Goosen had a series of choice words for the Travelers as he walked to first, and before he could reach the base, Arkansas catcher Sonny Ruberto rushed up the line and jumped on him. This time, the benches emptied, with players from both teams battling all over the infield. The *Arkansas Gazette* reported that there was a pile of twelve players at one point, as well as individual struggles all over the infield. One fan saw Arkansas pitcher Santiago Guzman knock down four Memphis players at home plate. Little Rock police eventually carried Guzman back to the dugout and herded the Blues back to theirs. Hepler was stretched out on the field, dazed.

As for Medwick, he told the *Gazette* that he had a hard time staying in the stands during the melee. "That's like the old Gas House Gang," he said.

"When a man hits a couple of home runs, what do they expect?" Memphis manager Roy Sievers told the Gazette. "They do it in the majors and everywhere. They retaliated and we didn't say anything. Tempers got hot, and that goes for both sides. It's part of the game. That's what makes it a great game."

Memphis catcher Lloyd Flodin wasn't as thrilled as his manager. "Four dollars a day isn't enough meal money for that," he told the *Gazette*.

Hepler came back to pitch the bottom of the sixth, but the Travelers won the game 6–4 to clinch the division. They lost to El Paso, three games to one in the championship series. At least the '34 Cardinals came away with a championship.

=43=
EL PASO AND THE
10-RUN GAME

EL PASO TRIED AND TRIED TO GET INTO THE TEXAS LEAGUE
before finally getting an invitation in the fall of 1961. Its team, the
Sun Kings, responded by dominating the league's statistics—at
least the hitting statistics—for the next decade.

Geography was a big part of the reason. El Paso was the highest city ever to have a Texas League team, at an elevation of more
than four thousand feet. Its windy desert climate and the hitter-
friendly dimensions at Dudley Field also made it a haven for batters. And it didn't hurt that the parent club, the San Francisco
Giants, sent some sluggers to its new affiliate, including Charlie
Dees, Dick Dietz, Jerry Robinson, and Winston Llenas. Jesus
Alou, one of three brothers of the famous Alou family, also played
for the Sun Kings.

From 1962 to 1970, El Paso hitters led the league in runs batted in six times, doubles five times, total bases five times, runs
scored five times, home runs four times, and batting average three
times. Double-figure scores were a staple at the "Dudley Dome,"
the team's adobe-block ballpark.

But the team that led in so many statistical categories also performed a rare statistical feat. On April 25, 1970, El Paso beat
Shreveport, 10–9, scoring one run in each of the ten innings. El

Paso had 15 hits in the game, including 3 by catcher Randy Niles and 2 by five others, including leadoff man Mickey Rivers.

Shreveport scored its runs in clusters, with 4 in the third, 1 in the fifth, and 4 more in the top of the ninth to take a 9–8 lead. But as the *El Paso Times* reported it, "The Kings scored their customary tally in the bottom of the ninth to send it to overtime." In the bottom of the tenth, Niles walked with one away, and one out later Jerry Feldman also walked, moving Niles to second. Rich Shibley then singled, and Niles scampered home with the winning run.

The *Times* reported just 633 in attendance for the game, as interest in the team seemed to have bottomed out after a long, hard stretch in the late 1960s. It wasn't for lack of excitement that year—Rivers led the league in hitting (.343), hits (tied with 154), slugging percentage (.537), and runs scored (99), and shortstop Billy Parker hit .312 with 21 homers. El Paso was competitive, finishing with the second-best record in the league behind Albuquerque.

El Paso did not have a team in 1971, sitting out a year before the Los Angeles Dodgers came to the rescue and moved their Double-A team from Albuquerque to El Paso (Albuquerque became a Triple-A franchise).

=44=
GREG ARNOLD

GREG ARNOLD HAD TALENT. EVEN THOUGH HE SIGNED WITH the Orioles out of Baltimore's Southern High School in 1966, he is still remembered as one of the hardest-throwing pitchers to come from the area.

Arnold had other talents as well. While he was in the minor leagues, he recorded several songs under the name El Fago Baco, and his performances as an Elvis Presley and Tom Jones impersonator earned him a gig in Las Vegas.

But in the late 1960s, he was known for a fastball that could reach one hundred miles an hour, one that made umpires nervous because it was so fast and had so much movement. Baseball Hall of Famer Jim Palmer, who was coming up through the Orioles' farm system at the time, once said he wished he had Arnold's arm. But Arnold often struggled to control the heater. After going 6–0 in the Appalachian League in 1967, he was a combined 12–10 in the Florida State and California Leagues in 1968 and 8–5 in the California and Texas leagues in 1969.

He was 5–3 with a 5.37 ERA the night of June 13, 1970, when he started on the mound for the Dallas–Fort Worth Spurs against the Memphis Blues at Arlington's Turnpike Stadium. He was down 2–0 in the third inning when he walked the Blues' Curt

Brown. He was behind in the count to the next hitter, Ted Bashore, when he looked at first and then appeared to stumble out of his stretch. Both umpires—Ernie Gallagher behind the plate and Nick Emetrio in the field—signaled a balk. Arnold yelled, "That was no [expletive] balk," then raced over to Emetrio, who was near second base, pushed him down, and began pummeling him. Stunned teammates pulled Arnold off the umpire, who was knocked out briefly, apparently from the initial fall. Emetrio was taken off the field in an ambulance and spent the night in an Arlington hospital but recovered completely.

Arnold suffered more lasting damage. League president Bobby Bragan, who lived in Fort Worth, was called to the ballpark, and he immediately suspended Arnold for the rest of the season, with the blessing of the Dallas–Fort Worth management and the Orioles.

For all his offbeat off-field activities, Arnold had never before been tossed out of a game. He apologized profusely in the media in the days after the incident. "I didn't mean to hit him or run over him, but I did and there's no excuse," Arnold told the *Dallas Morning News*. "Whatever punishment Mr. Bragan hands out is justified and I can't complain." "I don't know what happened," he was quoted as saying in the *Sporting News*. "Something snapped."

Arnold did not pitch again in 1970, but in 1971 he threw a no-hitter for Triple-A Rochester against Charleston. A game story from that day, May 28, 1971, referred to him as the "flamboyant fastball pitcher with irregular control," and the stats proved it—he walked five and struck out nine in the seven-inning game. The no-hitter turned out to be the highlight of his career, though, as he suffered an arm injury and never made it to the major leagues.

Never one to miss a chance at publicity for the Texas League, Bragan came up with a novel solution when the umpire Emetrio was ordered to take a few days off. Bragan hired veteran Fort

Worth umpire Ed Oliver, who had called hundreds of semipro and amateur games, as a temporary replacement. "If anyone wants to protest to him, he'll have to bring along a pencil and paper," Bragan told the *Sporting News*. The reason: Oliver was deaf.

=45=
TOM WALKER

TOM WALKER WASN'T THINKING ABOUT THROWING A NO-
hitter as the game between the Dallas–Fort Worth Spurs and the
Albuquerque Dodgers began on the night of August 4, 1971. In
fact, Walker wasn't thinking about anything. He was asleep on the
training room table in the visitors' clubhouse of Sports Stadium
when his teammates went to bat against the Dodgers' Jim Haller
in the top of the first. Walker had warmed up for his regular start,
but it had been raining, and he expected the game to be canceled.

"My roommate, Wayne Garland, came in and he says 'Walker,
aren't you going to pitch?'" Walker said in a feature in the baseball
magazine the *National Pastime.* "There was like an out in the top of
the first inning. I said 'I thought we were rained out.' He says 'No,
you better get your butt out there. The game's going on.'" Walker
threw on his uniform, raced out for a few brief warm-up throws,
and then proceeded to pitch one of the Texas League's greatest
games—a fifteen-inning no-hitter, the longest in league history.

The Baltimore Orioles' first-round draft pick in 1968, Walker
had shown promise before that soggy August night in New
Mexico. He was 8–8 with a 2.81 ERA in the California League in
1970, earning a promotion to the Dixie Association—a one-year
merger of the Texas and Southern leagues—for 1971. He was

9–6 going into the game against the Dodgers, with an ERA well under 3.00.

He had a perfect game through six innings, then walked Larry Eckenrode to start the bottom of the seventh. Eckenrode tried to steal to get into scoring position but was thrown out in the attempt. Walker then walked Lee Lacy but got a double play on a line drive to second baseman Rich Emard to end the inning. "That ballpark had a great big scoreboard," Walker said in the *National Pastime.* "I looked out there and all I could see were zeroes. The seventh came along and I thought holy cow, we have a chance here." The Dodgers got a man as far as second base in the eighth on a walk and a sacrifice, but after an intentional walk, both runners were stranded.

Walker did not allow a base runner after the eighth, retiring twenty-two in a row. In the eleventh, third baseman Steve Green made a bare-handed pickup on a slow roller and threw out Bob Cummings. In the fourteenth, left fielder Mike Reinbach made the defensive play of the game, catching the ball almost by accident. Reinbach—who had caught a fly ball with his back against the fence in the fifth—was tying his shoe when Cummings hit a sinking line drive to lead off the inning. The left fielder got a jump on the ball, then slipped on the wet grass and had to make a diving, one-handed catch. "That was the biggest play of the game," Walker said. "He'd have had an easy chance, really, but he slipped on the wet turf. He had to make a circus catch because he was so far off-balance when he slipped."

Walker was pitching a great game, but the Spurs weren't scoring any runs. Haller, a nineteen-year-old phenom, gave up nine hits in fourteen innings, but he stranded runners in scoring position in six innings and got out of a bases-loaded jam in the thirteenth. Haller finally came out after fourteen innings, as Dodgers manager Monty Basgall wanted to protect the young pitcher's arm. Spurs manager Cal Ripken Sr. was ready to pull Walker moments later. "He came down with two outs in the top of the 15th and said 'Tom, I can't let you go anymore. This is it,'" Walker said. "I didn't want to hear that, but I understood what he was saying." As the impact of the decision was sinking in, reliever Dave Allen walked Reinbach. The next batter, Enos Cabell, worked Allen to a 3–2 count, and then, with Reinbach breaking from first, Cabell cracked a double to center to score Reinbach with the game's only run. Ripken relented and gave Walker the ball for the bottom of the fifteenth. He retired the side in order in the bottom of the inning, getting a groundout from Lacy to end the game on his 176th pitch.

The crowd, which had grown from just over one thousand to double that as word of the game spread, gave Walker a standing ovation. The Dodgers organization sent a bottle of champagne to the Spurs' clubhouse. "There are a lot of things I'll remember about this night," Walker told the *Sporting News*. "One of the most unusual things was the emotional release afterward. I've never seen guys get so worked up after a game."

The no-hitter saved Walker's career. Feeling he was stuck behind the best pitching staff in baseball—the Orioles had four twenty-game winners in 1971—he had already enrolled at the University of Florida, planning to get his master's degree. With the resulting publicity from the no-hitter—not to mention a 13–9 record with a 2.25 ERA for the year—Walker was drafted by the Montreal Expos during the off-season and made it to the big leagues in 1972. "That no-hitter created a situation where it opened the eyes of other major-league teams, the Expos specifically," Walker said. "It propelled me from Double-A to the big leagues, got me off the ground. It changed my life."

Walker wound up pitching in 191 big-league games, going 18–23. He also had three more outstanding minor-league seasons, including a year with Denver in the American Association, where he went 7–0 with a 1.97 ERA. But nothing ever matched the fifteen-inning no-hitter, the one he almost missed because of a nap.

=HOME=

A REVIVAL

=46=
JIM PAUL

JIM PAUL IS THE FIRST ONE TO ADMIT THAT HE KNEW VERY little about minor-league baseball when be bought a small part of the El Paso Sun Kings before the 1974 season. But in some ways, that was a good thing.

Paul was sports information director at Southwestern Louisiana University when Wayne Vandenburg, an old friend from El Paso, called and asked him to become the Sun Kings' general manager and join a group called El Paso Professional Sports that was buying the team. Paul was waiting to hear from the university about a promotion to associate athletic director, but the call never came, so he moved to El Paso.

Attendance had been dismal in 1973, just 63,081, so the new owners were open to new ideas. They turned Paul loose, and he responded with a string of innovations, many of them revolutionary for baseball at the time.

He suggested a name change, offering three options. The ownership group chose "Diablos." He discovered a blackboard one of the previous owners had used to plan promotional events, and he filled it up, cooking up something for virtually every game. And he hired Brooklyn-born Paul Strelzin as the public-address announcer at the team's ballpark, Dudley Field. Strelzin, given free rein by Paul, used what one writer called a "blatant, strident style" to lead cheers and work up excitement in the ballpark. His cheer-leading led at least one manager to complain to Texas League president Bobby Bragan, in a conversation reported in Bob Ingram's book *Baseball: From Browns to Diablos*, a history of the game in El Paso:

> "Has Strelzin's announcing physically harmed any of your players?" Bragan asked the manager.
>
> "No," the manager answered.
>
> "Has it increased attendance?" Bragan asked.
>
> "Yes," he replied.
>
> "Then I recommend you try the Strelzin system," suggested Bragan, himself something of a promoter.

Paul had the stands at Dudley Field painted a bright yellow. Fans coming in the gates were each handed a tissue, the better to wave goodbye to a departing visiting pitcher—who was serenaded with Janis Joplin wailing "Bye Bye, Baby" on the PA system. The Diablos staged cow-milking contests and celebrity softball events between games of doubleheaders. And one day the club built what was billed as the world's largest banana split, 4 inches wide by 120 feet long, which was summarily consumed by hundreds of kids armed with Diablos-issued spoons.

El Paso responded, as attendance almost doubled, and Paul was named the Texas League Executive of the Year and the *Sporting News* Minor-League Executive of the Year.

Still, the club lost money, and El Paso Professional Sports was $52,000 in the hole. When a buyer for the team backed out just three weeks before the 1975 season opener, Paul went out and borrowed enough money to buy the whole operation. He managed to keep creditors at bay with payments of anywhere from $50 to $100 as the season progressed. He signed up a local radio station to carry Diablos home games. He encouraged Strelzin to become even more demonstrative, and the announcer responded by coming up with two flags—a red one to wave to stop opposing teams' rallies and a green one to encourage El Paso rallies. Strelzin gave all the players nicknames. One night, he introduced Allen Newsome as "Brahma Bull," and then bellowed like a bull. A fan in the bleachers bellowed back, and Strelzin observed, "Folks, I've found myself a mate."

Attendance soared again, this time to 162,399, by far the best in the league. Paul was honored by the league and the *Sporting News* for the second straight year. In 1975, Paul introduced fireworks displays to the ballpark, and attendance continued to grow. In 1977, crowds topped 200,000 for the first time in El Paso history.

As he was starting a revolution in minor-league baseball, Paul was also sharing his ideas in an annual conference of minor-league executives. The El Paso Promotional Seminar started with six people in 1974, a forum for sharing ideas about how to get fans into the seats. At its height in the 1980s, the seminar attracted more than two hundred executives, who shared ideas on everything from radio rights to nachos. "The ideas you got out of those meetings were amazing," Paul told *Baseball America* magazine in 2001 when the publication named him one of the most influential people in minor-league baseball history. "Every year it just astounded me with the young people who came up with great new ideas. And the disciples of the El Paso Seminar were going out and kicking butt."

Paul sold the Diablos in 1998 and the promotional seminar soon afterward, but his influence on the game continues. "In the '60s, baseball sat on its ass and said, 'We're the national pastime; come see us.' So what happens? Attendance dwindles and the '70s become a hotbed for NFL football," he once said. "No one bothered to call attention to baseball. We still had the older generation. They'd come forever. But we'd lost the younger generation, who didn't remember this was the national pastime. They had a lot of other ways to spend their time."

Paul figured out a way to get them back—and transformed how the game was promoted and produced.

=47=
BILL VALENTINE

WHEN BILL VALENTINE WAS NAMED THE GENERAL MANAGER
of the Arkansas Travelers—a team he had grown up watching—
he knew he had to make a big impact right away. He did that by
thinking small.

In February 1976, Valentine announced to anyone who would
listen that he was going to have a leadoff hitter in his first game
who was even shorter than the 3-foot-7 Eddie Gaedel who made
history when he pinch-hit for Bill Veeck's St. Louis Browns in
1951. Of course, there was one problem. Valentine didn't know
anyone in Little Rock who was smaller than Gaedel.

But one afternoon in March, Valentine was alone in the team's
offices when he heard the front door open and close. He could see
the door from his desk, but the bottom three feet of the view was
blocked by a counter. Valentine was about ready to look for ghosts
of Travelers past when Roscoe Steadman appeared around the
corner of the counter and announced that he was Valentine's
leadoff guy.

But Valentine—whose flair for promotions was to become legendary—couldn't just leave it at a little person leading off. So he
arranged for Steadman to be thrown out of the game after his at-
bat, which of course was going to produce a walk. And he saw

even more opportunities when a woman not much bigger than Steadman showed up in the Travelers' offices a couple of weeks later. Valentine gave her a part in the bit, too. On opening night, Steadman led off the game, to the delight of the crowd at Ray Winder Field. He walked. Then he was tossed from the game by the umpire, who at 6-foot-4 almost had to get on his hands and knees to argue with Steadman. Finally, for the coup de grâce, Steadman's "wife" in the bit raced onto the field, whacked the umpire in the rear end with a giant overstuffed purse (which had been supplied by Valentine), then fled for the dugout. The crowd howled, and Valentine's reputation began to build.

So did the crowds. The Travelers drew 67,473 fans in 1975, the year before Valentine took over. Attendance topped 100,000 in 1977 and 200,000 in 1980. Valentine was named the Texas League Executive of the Year in 1976, 1977, and 1978.

The former American League umpire helped revive the career of Captain Dynamite, who lost his job blowing himself up at Joey Chitwood's auto shows when the stunt tour folded. Valentine agreed to pay Captain Dynamite $500 to blow himself up at Ray Winder Field on consecutive weekends. The promotion turned out to be popular, and Captain Dynamite eventually became an attraction at ballparks from coast to coast.

Valentine's reputation even earned him credit for bits he didn't orchestrate. One season, a local savings and loan invited all the members of its Squirrel Club—set up for kids to learn the value of "squirreling away" money—to on-field activities before a game. During the festivities a live squirrel appeared at the top of the netting behind home plate and raced almost down to the field. When spotted, the skittish squirrel of course bolted back up the net, and fans and sports writers got a good laugh at Valentine's stunt. As Valentine said later, he didn't have anything to do with it, but he wasn't going to admit it. "A good promoter takes credit for everything," he said with a laugh.

Valentine's promotional skills have sometimes overshadowed his other roles with the Travelers. He has worked tirelessly to keep the community-owned team afloat in a one of the league's smallest markets, and he has labored to bring as many central Arkansas folks as possible into Ray Winder Field, the historic ballpark that opened in 1932, the year he was born.

Valentine began working at Ray Winder Field before he was ten, picking up seat cushions and sorting soda bottles. He later graduated to clubhouse boy—which consisted of hanging out players' sweaty uniforms to dry in the sun—and gradually worked his way into umpiring local baseball games. When he graduated from high school in 1950, Valentine was offered a scholarship at Arkansas Teachers College. Instead, he went to Bill McGowan's umpire school in Florida and zoomed to the head of the class. At the age of eighteen, he landed a job in the Ohio-Indiana League, becoming the youngest umpire in professional baseball history. He worked his way up to the American League in 1963 and labored there for five years before he lost his job in a dispute with the league over the formation of a union.

Fortunately for Little Rock and Arkansas, he returned home to work in radio and television with the Travelers, and in 1976 he was put in charge of the team. Things have never been the same. "Nobody was doing all these promotions at the time, except for [El Paso's] Jim Paul and me," Valentine said.

Paul's promotional seminars helped spread his ideas, and for years Valentine was in charge of a similar seminar at the meetings of the National Association. Together, they helped change the face of minor-league baseball. All it had needed was a little promotion.

=48=
DAVE RIGHETTI

AMONG THE 226 PEOPLE IN THE STANDS AT TULSA'S dilapidated Driller Park on the afternoon of July 16, 1978, was a scout for the New York Yankees, Jerry Walker. Walker probably wasn't there to see the starting pitcher, a nineteen-year-old kid who had been shelled in his last start and who had missed the past month and a half of the season with a groin injury. But he left the park knowing the left-hander's name: Dave Righetti. On that blistering hot Sunday afternoon, Righetti struck out twenty-one Midland Cubs hitters, breaking a sixty-nine-year-old Texas League record for strikeouts in a nine-inning game.

Righetti had been the Texas Rangers' number one draft pick the year before, and he had worn out Class A hitters, going 11–3 after signing with the Rangers. Once he came off the disabled list the next summer, he showed the same kind of ability—in the seven starts before his gem on July 16, he had struck out at least ten four times. But his last start had been a bad one—six runs in three innings—and he had been chewed out by Tulsa manager Marty Martinez. So expectations for the hurler might have gone down, but not for long.

In the first inning, Righetti struck out two batters. He struck out the side in the second and third and added two more in the fourth. Two more went down in the fifth, just one in the sixth, and two more in the seventh, for a total of fifteen. Midland scored a run in the seventh when Tulsa right fielder Dave Rivera—who had forgotten his sunglasses—lost a fly ball by the Cubs' Eric Grandy in the sun, allowing Grandy to reach second. A single brought him home, but Tulsa still led 2–1.

Righetti struck out the side in the eighth, but Steve Macko led off the Midland ninth with a double (Righetti later admitted he hung a slider to the Cubs shortstop, who was the only Midland player not to strike out). Two strikeouts later, Kevin Drury singled in Macko with the tying run. Righettti got another strikeout to get out of the inning and break the league record, but all he could think about on the way to the dugout was that he had given up the tying run. "I had tears in my eyes because I thought I had let the team down, because we didn't win," Righetti told the *Tulsa World* years later. "I wanted to be a winner, and we were having a tough time."

Reliever Steve Bianchi gave up two runs in the top of the tenth, and Midland got the 4–2 victory. All Righetti got was the record.

"That was the greatest game I've seen," Rangers pitching instructor Dick Such said after the game. Righetti's 21 strikeouts gave him 100 for the season in 68 innings. He threw 140 pitches, an amazing number for a minor-leaguer today but still not uncommon in the 1970s. "I felt comfortable out there," he said after the game. "I had all my pitches, fastball, curve, slider and changeup. I was using a different motion because I wanted to slow myself down and not overthrow. I blocked out everything and concentrated on throwing strikes."

The game turned out to be one of the last the left-hander threw that season. After three more starts, the Rangers sidelined him for the season because of tendinitis in his bicep. He finished the season with 127 strikeouts in 91 innings and a 5–5 record.

That fall, Rangers owner Brad Corbett was working on a trade to get Yankees pitcher Sparky Lyle. As negotiations wore down, Yankees owner George Steinbrenner took some advice from his scout, Jerry Walker, and asked for the young pitcher to be thrown in to complete the ten-player deal. "George told me I wasn't part of the deal, that he just pulled my name out of his pocket," Righetti said. "Jerry Walker had told him just to ask for this kid— the worst thing they could do was say no. It was a big deal, but it just wasn't about me. They [the Rangers] basically thought I was sore-armed so they went ahead and took a chance by trading me."

However, the Yankees knew what they were getting. "He's the big man in the deal for us," Yankees president Al Rosen told the *Sporting News* after the trade. "We're all in love with him. Jerry Walker, who was with [Yankees ace Ron] Guidry in the beginning, thinks we have another Guidry."

The Yankees were right. Righetti was the American League Rookie of the Year in 1981, and he was 2–1 in the postseason as the Yankees went to the World Series. He went on to throw a no-hitter in 1983, and in 1984 he moved to the bullpen. As the Yankees' closer, he won the league's Fireman of the Year award twice and went seven straight years with at least 20 saves, including a major-league record 46 in 1986.

His 21-strikeout game is still a Texas League record.

=49=
MIKE REMLINGER

THE REASON THE SAN FRANCISCO GIANTS DRAFTED MIKE Remlinger in the first round of the 1987 draft would soon become obvious. He spent two days at Everett in the Northwest League and struck out 11 batters in five innings. He moved up to the Midwest League and struck out 43 in 31 innings. At Double-A Shreveport, where he finished the season, he struck out 51 in 34⅓ innings, went 4–2, and had an ERA of 2.36.

It was in his third start for the Shreveport Captains that his potential became most evident. On August 12, on the mound at home against the Tulsa Drillers, Remlinger struck out the side in the first inning. He did the same thing in the second. And the third. When George Threadgill flied out to center to start the fourth inning, it was a moral victory for the Drillers. The out also prevented Remlinger from tying the Texas League record of ten strikeouts to start a game, a record set by Harry Ables in 1910.

Still, the Drillers could not touch Remlinger. When Shreveport manager Jack Mull took him out of the game after seven innings—he had reached his pitch limit of 120—Remlinger had recorded fifteen strikeouts and had walked just one batter. He had also not allowed a hit. The Captains' bullpen eventually gave up a hit, losing the no-hitter, but Remlinger got the win.

Remlinger was injured for most of the next season but worked his way to the major leagues for the first time in 1991, when he appeared in eight games for the San Francisco Giants. He bounced through the Giants, New York Mets, and Cincinnati Reds organizations before finally getting a chance at a full season with the Reds in 1997. Since then, he has become one of the game's steadiest set-up men, for the Atlanta Braves from 1999 to 2002 and for the Chicago Cubs in 2003. And while he hasn't gone on any more nine-strikeout-in-a-row tears, he still averages almost a strikeout an inning.

=50=
EL PASO 35,
BEAUMONT 21

EL PASO'S DUDLEY FIELD—WHERE THE AIR WAS THIN, THE
prevailing winds blew out to right, and the desert wind tended to
turn the infield to concrete—always had a reputation as a hitter-
friendly ballpark. But what happened on April 30, 1983, in a game
between the El Paso Diablos and the Beaumont Golden Gators
was extraordinary even for Dudley Field.

After one inning, El Paso led 6–3. After three, it was 10–7. So
far, nothing that unusual. But Beaumont went up 11–10 in the
fourth, then scored 3 more in the fifth, a single run in the sixth,
and 3 more in the seventh and ninth, for a grand total of 21. And
they lost by 14.

"This ballpark is just absolutely electric," Diablos manager
Tony Muser told the *El Paso Times* after the 35–21 game, which
broke Texas League records for total runs, runs batted in, and hits.
"That's the only way I can explain it." Nature—and the grounds-
keepers—helped a little, too. The relative humidity was 7 percent,
and the wind was gusting up to thirty-five miles an hour to right
field that night. And the infield was extra-hard because of an
additive the team had used to help dry out the dirt after an early
season snowstorm. Balls hit on the ground either scooted through
the infield so fast they couldn't be handled, or they ate up the

OTHER BIG INNINGS AND BIG GAMES

The history of the Texas League is littered with big comebacks, explosive innings, and high-scoring games. Some are the result of the conditions—such as the altitude and wind in Midland and El Paso—and some are just the result of bad pitching, back luck, or bad defense.

One of the biggest innings came early in league history, when the league was still struggling to survive. On April 27, 1895, Shreveport scored fourteen runs in the fifth inning of a game against Sherman and wound up winning 21–20.

Houston player–manager George Reed sparked an 11-run fourth-inning rally against San Antonio in 1898. The Buffs managed 23 hits—Reed had 5 of them—in coming back from a 4–1 deficit to win 24–11.

In 1925, Fort Worth scored 10 runs in the fifth inning of a 29–9 pasting of San Antonio. "It was probably the worst drubbing that was ever administered to a San Antonio team rated as a championship contender," the *San Antonio Express* groused. The day before, the Cats' Ziggy Sears had driven in 11 runs in Fort Worth's 19–8 romp over the Bears. And the next day, Fort Worth won 24–12 to complete a sweep of the series. In that game, San Antonio pitcher Bob Couchman and a policeman named O'Banion served as umpires after the original pair left the game under police protection.

On May 5, 1983, with wind gusts of up to thirty-five miles an hour blowing out of Midland's Christensen Stadium, the hometown Cubs scored 11 runs in the bottom of the first against El Paso. Fifteen batters came to the plate, with three of them getting 2 hits each. In the top of the second, the Diablos sent 17 men to the plate—13 of them got hits—and went ahead 13–11. Midland answered with 5 more in the bottom of the inning to make it 16–13. El Paso scored 4 more in the third, and the score was 17–16 after three innings. Fortunately, the winds died down a little and some semblance of pitching returned. El Paso won, 20–19, with a run in the top of the ninth.

On June 15, 1998, Arkansas rallied from deficits of 4–0, 9–4, and 20–13 to beat Jackson 21–20 on a homer by Tyrone Horne in the bottom of the tenth. The teams combined for 49 hits, 20 of them for extra bases. "I've never seen anything like that in my life," Arkansas manager Chris Maloney told *Baseball America*.

Later that summer, Wichita went to the eleventh inning in a scoreless tie with San Antonio, and the Wranglers had the usually dependable Steve Prihoda on the mound. Before the half-inning was over, the Missions had scored 12 runs on 10 hits, including a grand slam and a solo homer by San Antonio catcher Angel Pena, who went 5 for 5 on the night. ★

infielders, who were charged with 8 errors. Balls hit in the air soared toward the fences—there were 10 doubles and 8 home runs.

El Paso center fielder Mike Felder had nine RBIs, coming on a grand slam, a three-run homer, a sacrifice fly, and, incredibly considering the conditions, a sacrifice bunt. The Diablos' Jim Paciorek, struggling through an 0-for-9 streak going into the game, went 6 for 7. El Paso right fielder Stan Levi scored seven times.

"I was happy whenever somebody made an out," Muser told *Baseball America* magazine. "Heck, I don't think Nolan Ryan would have gotten anybody out that night. "The pitchers? They were just sick. They didn't know what to do." Beaumont resorted to backup shortstop Dan Pupura in relief. He gave up 11 runs and 10 hits in three innings. The Diablos' winning pitcher, Bob Schroeck, allowed 7 runs on 7 hits in four innings.

The run production more or less returned to normal the next night. Beaumont scored 11 runs in the top of the first but added just 9 more and went on to win 20–13.

=51=
THE 1994 MIRACLE

THE TEXAS LEAGUE PLAYOFFS HAVE NEVER LACKED FOR dramatic moments, from Charlie Gorin's no-hitter to win the 1959 Pan American Series to the nineteen-inning duel between Fort Worth and Shreveport in the 1942 postseason to the heroics of aging San Antonio pitcher Procopio Herrera in the 1950 Dixie Series. But for pure drama, few games can match the fifth and deciding game of the East Division playoffs in 1994.

The evenly matched Shreveport Captains and Jackson Generals had split their regular-season games, winning sixteen each. In their postseason series, they had played a tense four games leading up to the afternoon of September 3, at Jackson's Smith-Willis Stadium.

The Captains' Shad Smith, who had been just 6–9 for Shreveport in the regular season, dominated the Generals all day. He did not allow a base runner until Fletcher Thompson singled with two out in the sixth, and he allowed just one other hit, by Tom Nevers, in the seventh, through the first 8⅔ innings.

Jackson's Jim Waring was nearly as good. The only run he gave up came in the top of the first, when the relay to first on a double-play ball pulled Dennis Colon off the base. In the top of the ninth, the Captains loaded the bases with two out and Smith coming to the plate. Shreveport manager Ron Wotus faced a dilemma—let Smith, who was pitching so well, hit for himself and stay in the game, or take him out and try to score more runs. Wotus decided to let Smith stay in the game and take his chances at the plate. The pitcher grounded out to end the inning.

Smith retired the first two Jackson batters in the bottom of the ninth to bring up Nevers, the Generals' shortstop, who had hit just .267 with eight homers during the regular season. Smith got a strike on the first pitch. The next pitch was a fastball on the outside corner, and Nevers hit a long fly ball to right. The ball kept carrying, landing just over the fence for a game-tying home run.

Following the homer, Wotus brought in closer Stacy Jones, who had led the league in saves that year with thirty-four. His job was to retire Jackson's best hitter, third baseman Jeff Ball, and avoid facing power-hitting cleanup man Bobby Abreu, who was on deck. Ball, who led the Generals with a .316 average in the regular season, got ahead 2–0 in the count. He was looking for a fastball on the next pitch, and he got one, ripping it toward the sixteen-foot wall in center field, four hundred feet away. As the ball cleared the wall, the Jackson players stormed onto the field. Team manager Sal Butera, who had been in the third-base coach's box, ran arm-in-arm with Ball from third base to the plate. "I swung, and a great thing happened," Ball told the *Jackson Clarion-Ledger* after the game. "This is just the biggest thrill of my life. And to do it here—it's just unbelievable."

Nevers was crying as he watched Ball's homer soar beyond the fence and said, "There is nothing to compare to this, nothing ever."

The elation wore off quickly, though, as Jackson faced El Paso, which had won both half-seasons in the West Division, in the league championship series. El Paso pitching shut out Jackson in the first game of the championship series, and the Diablos went on to a four-game sweep.

Nevers, who had been a first-round draft pick by the Astros in 1990, stayed in baseball through the 2002 season but never made it to the majors. Ball made it briefly, appearing in two games for the San Francisco Giants in 1998.

=52=
SAN ANTONIO 1, JACKSON 0, 26 INNINGS

FOR DECADES, THE TEXAS LEAGUE HAS HAD A REPUTATION as a hitters' league, thanks in part to the effects of altitude and prevailing winds in the West Texas outposts of El Paso and Midland and to the hitter-friendly fences in Wichita and Tulsa. But San Antonio has never shared in that reputation. As one bitter San Antonio batter once observed, "This is where fly-ball hitters go to die." Both V. J. Keefe Field, the team's home from 1968 to 1993, and Wolff Stadium, the team's present ballpark, were designed to have the prevailing summer winds blow in from the outfield.

Of all the long nights inflicted on hitters in the last thirty-five years, though, the longest was the night of Thursday, July 14, 1988, and the wee hours of Friday, July 15. For twenty-five innings, the San Antonio Missions and the Jackson Mets slugged it out—well, figuratively—at V. J. Keefe Field without scoring a run. For seven hours and ten minutes, they battled futility. "You could have a bad week on a night like this," Jackson play-by-play man Bill Walberg cracked.

A crowd of 3,792 was at the game initially, one of the biggest of the season. By midnight, it had dwindled to 321 die-hard fans. The Missions' front office went out and bought a round of coffee, doughnuts, and breakfast tacos for those who remained. An all-night talk radio station in New York called the front office, wanting details. Walberg ran out of major-league scores to report and started looking for Japan League results.

With the winds blowing in, the chances for a game-ending home run were all but nil, which led both teams to take extra chances on the bases. In the fifth and twenty-fourth innings, San Antonio third baseman Walt McConnell threw out runners trying to score from third. The Missions' Mike Huff led off the twenty-first inning with a double but was thrown out trying to stretch it to a triple.

The managers—Kevin Kennedy for San Antonio and Tucker Ashford for Jackson—almost depleted their rosters and had to leave pitchers in to hit for themselves in the late innings. The pitchers weren't successful at the plate either, although one should have been rested: the Missions' Barry Wohler, who flied out to left in the twenty-fifth, had slept from the sixteenth to the twenty-second innings.

Finally, at 2:25 A.M., the managers, the umpires, and Missions general manager Burl Yarbrough retreated to the team's offices to call Texas League president Carl Sawatski for advice. Awakened from a sound sleep in his home in Little Rock (he thought the call was a wrong number), Sawatski told Yarbrough to stop the game and pick it up later. The remaining handful of fans booed with all their sugar-induced might when the decision was announced at 2:30 A.M.

After allowing the teams to recover with just a nine-inning contest on July 15, the game resumed on Saturday, July 16. McConnell scored the winning run in the bottom of the twenty-sixth on an RBI single by Manny Francois. It had taken all of thirteen minutes to complete the longest game in Texas League history. Blaine Beatty was the losing pitcher for Jackson, but he made up for it by throwing a shutout in the regularly scheduled game that followed, winning 4–0. Oddly, Beatty allowed 1 run on 3 hits

LONGEST TEXAS LEAGUE GAMES

						INNINGS
San Antonio	1	Jackson	0	July 14–16, 1988		26
Austin	2	Dallas–Fort Worth	1	June 17, 1965		25
Rio Grande Valley	4	San Antonio	2	April 29, 1960		24
San Antonio	1	Waco	1	July 5, 1910		23
Tulsa	11	Jackson	7	July 6, 1982		23
Tulsa	6	Houston	5	August 16, 1952		22
Tulsa	3	Dallas	2	May 13, 1954		22
Arkansas	5	Dallas–Fort Worth	4	July 21, 1971		22
San Antonio	4	Dallas	3	June 2, 1935		21
Dallas	2	Oklahoma City	1	September 5, 1940		21
Shreveport	4	San Antonio	3	May 21, 1987		21
Midland	7	San Antonio	3	August 14, 2004		21
Waco	4	Galveston	1	August 13, 1916		20
Fort Worth	1	Shreveport	1	May 8, 1918		20
Fort Worth	4	Oklahoma City	3	May 31, 1939		20
Austin	4	Oklahoma City	3	May 29, 1956		20
Austin	4	Dallas	3	September 7, 1956		20
San Antonio	4	El Paso	3	June 28, 1977		20

in one third of an inning in the twenty-six-inning loss, then gave up just four hits and no runs in nine innings to pick up the win in the second game.

Not surprisingly, the game set a number of league records: longest game played to a decision (twenty-six innings), longest game by time (seven hours, twenty-three minutes), longest 1–0 game, most scoreless innings, and most strikeouts in a game by both teams (thirty-six).

=53=
RON ROENICKE

GOING INTO THE SPRING OF 1997, SAN ANTONIO HAD NOT
won a Texas League pennant in thirty-two years, at the time the
longest championship drought in the league.

There had been some close calls since Joe Morgan led the
Bullets to the title in 1964. After all, San Antonio had advanced
to the league championship series five times. But in 1973, the
Brewers lost the fifth and deciding game against Memphis. In
1979–81, the Dodgers were swept three straight times in the
championship series. And in 1990, the Missions had fallen to
Shreveport, four games to two. (The name of the San Antonio
team changed several times over this period.)

Since 1990, though, San Antonio had been awful. The
Missions had finished with the worst record in the league's West
Division four times from 1991 to 1996 and hadn't topped .500 in
any of those seasons. Managers came and went, and the parent
Los Angeles Dodgers stuck to a philosophy that de-emphasized
winning at the minor-league level. Young players who showed
flashes of ability were often promoted to Triple-A. Frequent player
moves made team-building difficult.

But a different kind of team came to San Antonio in 1997. The
1997 Missions had some of the Dodgers' top prospects, including

shortstop Alex Cora, the younger brother of big-league veteran Joey Cora, and center fielder Kevin Gibbs, who had stolen sixty bases the year before in Class A. They also had catcher Paul LoDuca, who had been a top prospect before injuries had derailed his career. At the same time, the Missions had a core of experienced players, including center fielder Garey Ingram, who had been to the major leagues, and six-year minor-league veteran first baseman Jay Kirkpatrick, who had driven in seventy-five runs for San Antonio in 1994. They also had J. P. Roberge, a utility man who had jumped from Class A to Triple-A in just three seasons in the minors.

But most important, the Dodgers sent one of their top managerial prospects to San Antonio in Ron Roenicke. A former number one draft pick of the Dodgers who had risen through the minors but never blossomed in the majors, Roenicke was the California League Manager of the Year in 1995 after leading San Bernardino—which featured many of the 1997 Missions players—to the pennant. Roenicke, who joked that he learned the game because he had to sit and watch so many from the dugout, turned out to be just as successful at the Double-A level as he had been in Class A.

Blessed with veteran pitching coach Guy Conti—who had waited eleven years for a promotion from Class A—and former big-league star Lance Parrish as his hitting coach, Roenicke's club started fast. At one point in late April and early May, the Missions won thirteen of fourteen to take control of the Texas League West.

Besides offense, the Missions were blessed with good pitching. Eric Weaver started the season 7–1, and nineteen-year-old Dennys Reyes, whose father had been a star in the Mexican League, won his first eight decisions.

And San Antonio seemed to be able to find ways to win. The Missions beat El Paso with a six-run seventh-inning rally the day they moved into first place. They won in the bottom of the ninth twice in the span of a week. By the end of May, they were 36–17, and eight different players had earned honors: Roberge, Ingram, and LoDuca had been the Texas League player of the week; Reyes and Weaver had shared the league's pitcher of the week honor; Roberge had been named the league's player of the month for May; Ignacio Flores, who started the season 6–2, was the Dodgers' minor-leaguer of the month; and Gibbs and third base-man Brian Richardson had been named Dodgers minor-leaguers of the week. Roberge hit .355 in May, and he showed his versatil-ity all season, playing first base, second base, left field, and catcher.

San Antonio clinched its first playoff berth since 1990 with 10 games left in the first half. But the Dodgers organization started making moves, as Reyes, Weaver, and Petie Roach, who had been 7–4 in the first half, were promoted to Triple-A.

After the flurry of changes, the Missions slumped to 6–10 at the start of the second half. Yet after the break for the Double-A All-Star game in July, San Antonio had one of those games that turn around seasons. The Missions trailed Arkansas 4–3 in the bottom of the ninth on July 14, with the Travelers' closer, Aaron Looper, on the mound. Cora led off with a double just inside the first-base bag. LoDuca had been on deck to pinch-hit, but Roenicke called him back and sent up Gibbs, a switch-hitter, to bat left-handed. Gibbs was coming off the injured list and could-n't even swing a bat left-handed, but Arkansas didn't know that. All the Travelers knew was that Gibbs was third in the league in hitting and was a tremendous bunter. Gibbs squared around to bunt on the first pitch, forcing the third baseman to charge in and leave the base uncovered. Gibbs waved at the ball and missed, but Cora stole third without a throw. Roenicke then sent LoDuca up to hit for Gibbs, and he singled to score the tying run. San Antonio went on to win the game on a bases-loaded walk in the twelfth inning.

The Missions stayed close to El Paso in the second half of the season, thanks to the addition of several new pitchers. Rick Gorecki, who had missed the entire 1995 and 1996 seasons with injuries, came in and became the ace of the staff. Left-hander Will Brunson joined the rotation, and screwball pitcher Jeff Kubenka, who had been a star for St. Mary's University in San Antonio the year before, came in as the closer.

The second-half title came down to the final series with the first-place Diablos. San Antonio could avoid a West Division series with the powerful Diablos—who had a team batting average over .300—by winning four of the five games at Cohen Stadium.

In the first game, Kubenka—who had been all but unhittable since joining the team in July—lost a two-run lead in the bottom of the ninth. But in the tenth, Richardson singled home Vernon Spearman for the go-ahead run, and Kubenka made it stand up. San Antonio took the second game 11–5 and the third 10–6. And then came the clincher, in front of one of the biggest crowds of the season at Cohen Stadium, 7,090.

El Paso led 5–1 going into the top of the eighth inning. With a run in, two on, and two out, Roenicke sent Keith Johnson up to pinch-hit for Cora. Johnson, who had been limited to a utility role with the emergence of the sure-handed Cora at short, wasn't at 100 percent that night in El Paso. He had sprained his ankle the week before when he ran into the wall at Wolff Stadium, so he wasn't able to run very well. But Roenicke depended on him in the clutch—Johnson had beaten Wichita with a pinch-hit single six days before. Johnson delivered again, hitting a game-tying homer. And he stayed in the game to play the outfield, despite his limited mobility.

El Paso went ahead again, 7–5, in the bottom of the eighth, but with one away in the top of the ninth, San Antonio put two runners on base, and Johnson came up again. He worked the count to 2–1, then ripped the next pitch to center field for a game-tying triple. He scored moments later on a sacrifice fly by Gibbs, and San Antonio held on for an 8–7 victory and the second-half title.

Shreveport, which had been just about as dominant in the East, also swept both halves, sending the playoffs directly to the championship series.

San Antonio won the first two games—the first playoffs ever at Wolff Stadium—by identical 6–0 scores. Roberge won the third game with a solo homer in the bottom of the ninth to send the Missions to Shreveport with a 3–0 lead. But the Captains, who had two of the league's top starters in Troy Brohawn and Bob Howry, used that tough pitching to stifle the Missions in the next three games and even the series.

That set up the deciding game between Brunson, who had been the Missions' best starter down the stretch, and Eddie Oropesa, a former Missions pitcher who had been tough on them all season.

Oropesa was tough again—San Antonio managed just two runs—but Brunson was better, pitching eight shutout innings. (He allowed just one earned run in two playoff appearances.) Kubenka pitched a scoreless ninth in relief, and San Antonio finally broke its championship drought with the 2–0 victory.

Almost to a man, the players credited Roenicke with making great game decisions and helping them refine their skills during pregame work. "I owe a lot to Ron," Johnson said. "The years I played for him, I started paying a whole lot more attention to the game. He had such a good eye about the game, things that most people would miss. I think playing for him made me a much more intelligent player. I became a player who would always be thinking about things that were going to happen, so I could react properly instead of everything being a surprise."

Parrish also benefited from working with Roenicke, a lifelong friend from Southern California. In 1998, when Roenicke was promoted from San Antonio to Triple-A Albuquerque at mid-season, Parrish took over the team and guided it through an injury- and promotion-depleted second half. San Antonio battled Wichita down to the wire in the first round of the playoffs before losing, three games to two.

The 1998 postseason appearance was the last for the Missions as a Dodgers farm club. After the 2000 season, their twenty-three-year relationship—which produced the single pennant in 1997—ended, as San Antonio signed on with the Seattle Mariners.

Roenicke went on to manage in Triple-A, and then when former Dodgers teammate Mike Scioscia was named manager of the Anaheim Angels, he was hired as bench coach. Parrish went on to work in the majors as well, as a coach for the Detroit Tigers.

=54=
TYRONE HORNE

TYRONE HORNE WAS NEVER ONE OF THOSE "FIVE-TOOL" players the scouts always dream about finding—the guys who can hit for average, hit for power, run, throw, and field. Horne was more of a 1½- tool player. He never earned mention for his defense or his baserunning prowess. In some of his thirteen seasons in the minor leagues, he hit for average. In all of them, though, he hit for power. Lots of power.

A forty-fourth-round draft pick by the Montreal Expos in 1989, Horne was with his fourth organization in 1998. The St. Louis Cardinals had decided to give him a shot at Double-A Arkansas after he had led the Florida Marlins' affiliate in the Midwest League in hitting (.306), home runs (21), runs batted in (91), and walks (104) in 1997. Horne stayed hot for the Travelers in 1998, with a batting average that hovered around .300 and a league-leading home run total, even before a once-in-a-lifetime night in San Antonio on July 27, the day before the Texas League All-Star break.

Batting third in the order for Arkansas, Horne connected on a two-run homer in the top of the first against Missions starter Peter Zamora. In the second, he came up with the bases loaded and launched an opposite-field shot onto the grassy berm in left

---

OTHER BIG PERFORMANCES

Tyrone Horne's "homer cycle" tops all the big-hitting days in Texas League history, but there have been plenty of other notable performances at the plate.

In 1961, Ardmore's Al Nagel hit 5 home runs and drove in 10 runs in a doubleheader in Amarillo. Nagel hit 4 of the homers in the second game, which Ardmore won 14–5, and he drove in 9 runs in the game. The 5 shots gave him 14 for the season and a share of the league lead on May 29, but he finished the season with just 20.

The next year, El Paso's first in the league, Sun Kings' first baseman Charlie Dees hit 4 home runs in 4 trips to the plate in an 11–3 romp over Amarillo. Dees hit a 3-run shot in the first, a 2-run homer in the second, and solo shots in the fourth and eighth. Dees was a solid hitter that season—he led the league in batting average (.348) and doubles (41), and he had 23 homers with 115 RBIs for the pennant-winning Sun Kings.

On June 18, 1980, another El Paso slugger hit four homers in a game. Tom Brunansky, at nineteen one of the youngest players in the league, hit three over the center field wall in Midland, with the fourth—which came in the fifth inning—just clearing the foul pole in left. The first two came with no wind at all; the last two had some help. With the game out of reach for the home team, Midland fans were cheering for Brunansky to add a fifth shot to his total as he came up in the seventh inning. But he flied out to center, then struck out and grounded out his next two times to the plate. Interestingly, the quartet of homers were his first since he hit his eighth of the season on May 23. ★

---

field, one of the toughest places in Wolff Stadium to hit one out. In the fifth, he hit a solo home run off Zamora, earning a standing ovation from the crowd and breaking a stadium record in a park where the wind almost always blows in on the hitters.

In the sixth, he came up against reliever Miguel Garcia with two runners on base. There was a buzz in the crowd, as some realized the significance of the moment. With a home run, Horne would accomplish what no other professional player—no other player at any level, from what anyone can tell—had done. A three-run homer would give him the cycle: a solo homer, a two-run homer, a three-run homer, and a grand slam. And when the ball he hit off Garcia cleared the left-field wall, the San Antonio fans bowed to his accomplishment and cheered. "Honestly, there's no explanation for this," Horne told the *San Antonio Express-News* after the game. "I was just in a groove. I didn't know what I was doing. I'm just shocked."

It was a shocking night. Besides the "homer cycle," Horne drove in ten runs, the first time a Texas Leaguer had reached double figures in almost forty years. He is just the sixth player in league history to drive in ten or more runs in a game.

The next day, he won the home run derby at the Texas League All-Star game, and he told the *Arkansas Democrat* that he hoped the attention from the "homer cycle" would get him a shot with the big-league club. But despite nationwide publicity, Horne did not get the call to the majors. He appeared in three games in Triple-A in 1998 but was released at the end of the season. He never reached even that level again, playing parts of two seasons at Double-A with two different organizations and a season of independent ball.

But wherever there are trivia quizzes—including the Baseball Hall of Fame's Web site—Tyrone Horne, the 1½-tool player who hit for the homer cycle will be remembered.

=55=
ALEX CABRERA
AND FRANK HOWARD

ALEX CABRERA CAME TO THE EL PASO DIABLOS AS DAMAGED goods in the spring of 2000. Having played for China Trust in Taiwan's Chinese Professional Baseball League in 1999, Cabrera was signed by the Arizona Diamondbacks during the Venezuelan winter season in 1999–2000. Five days after he signed, he hurt a disc in his back.

The injury prevented the twenty-seven-year-old Cabrera—who had already been playing professional baseball for nine seasons—from challenging for a job on the big-league club. He started the season at Triple-A, but the Tucson Toros opened the season in Canada, and the cool spring weather made it difficult for Cabrera to be able to loosen up and play every day. The Diamondbacks sent him to El Paso, in the warmer Texas League, at the end of April.

The move worked. On May 9, he homered against Arkansas. On May 10, he went 4 for 4 with 2 home runs and 5 runs batted in against the Travelers. On May 11, he went 3 for 5 with 2 homers and 5 runs batted in, also against Arkansas. On May 12, he hit 3 home runs off San Antonio's Allen Davis. On May 13, he hit another homer. And on May 14, he hit a dramatic home run to win the game in the bottom of the eleventh inning. In six games,

Cabrera hit 10 home runs and drove in 20 runs. During the streak, he hit a staggering .593 and scored 12 times. To put the streak into perspective, just six players in minor-league history have ever homered in more than six straight games.

And Cabrera was just getting started. On May 25, he drove in 6 runs with a pair of towering shots in Midland. Three days later, he had another 2-homer night, this time against Round Rock. In the month of May, Cabrera hit 21 home runs and drove in 50 runs, totals that are amazing for a month and are more than many players produce in a Double-A season. In all of minor-league history, only one player has had more RBIs in a month, and only one has recorded more home runs in a month.

The outburst started talk about some of the Texas League's greatest sluggers, including Ken Guettler, who hit a league-record 62 in 1956, and Clarence Kraft, who hit 55 in 1924. It also stirred up memories of one of the game's most feared sluggers, Frank Howard.

At 6 foot 8 and 255 pounds, Howard was a giant of a man. He came to the Texas League's Victoria Rosebuds in the spring of 1959 with just one season of professional experience—and 39 home runs—under his belt. In the first two months of the season, he crushed Texas League pitching, hitting 27 homers and driving in 79 runs.

His biggest day came in a doubleheader in Austin on June 8. In the first game, he drove in two runs with a double. In his first two at-bats in the second game, he drove in a run with a groundout in the first and struck out. In the fifth, with two men on, he hit a blast that cleared the center-field wall at Disch Field, more than 400 feet away. In the sixth he came up with two men on and roped a 354-foot opposite-field homer. In the seventh, again with two on, he ripped a 400-foot shot to left. He totaled 10 RBIs for the game and 12 for the doubleheader. He was shipped out to Triple-A soon thereafter, and the next season he was named the National

League Rookie of the Year after hitting 23 homers and driving in 77 runs in 117 games with the Los Angeles Dodgers.

Cabrera also earned a shot at the big leagues, called up to the Diamondbacks after hitting .382 with 35 homers and 82 RBIs in 53 games for El Paso. He hit .263 with 5 homers and 14 RBIs in 31 games in the majors, but he didn't stick with Arizona, as the Diamondbacks sold him to the Seibu Lions of Japan's Pacific League during the off-season. He responded once again by putting up monster power numbers. In 2001, he led the league with 49 home runs. In 2002, he tied Sadaharu Oh's record for homers in a season with 55 and to prevent him from breaking the record was not pitched to the entire final week of the season. In 2003, he hit 50 more.

Cabrera has expressed frustration at not getting more chances at the major leagues, scoffing at reports that he strikes out too much and can't hit a curveball. "If someone gives me a chance in the majors, I'll hit more than 40 jacks," he told espn.com in 2003. "If I have a chance to go back to America, I will. If someone calls me, I go." But even if he never gets another shot, his place in Texas League history is assured.

=56=
ERIC GAGNE

WHEN A HUSKY FRENCH CANADIAN FORMER HOCKEY PLAYER
named Eric Gagne showed up on the San Antonio Missions' roster at the end of the 1998 season, he did not attract a lot of attention. Sure, Gagne had posted good numbers at Class A Vero
Beach, going 9–7 with 144 strikeouts in 139⅔ innings, but he had
missed the entire 1997 season after surgery on his arm, and he was
still considered more of a thrower than a pitcher. In his only start
for the Missions in 1998, in the West Division playoffs against
Wichita, Gagne got a no-decision. But a year later, everyone in the
Texas League knew who he was: named as the league's best
pitcher, he had been called up to the major leagues.

Gagne impressed everyone in the Los Angeles Dodgers' organization in the spring of 1999, making him an easy choice to start
for the Missions on opening day. And while that game wasn't particularly memorable, the next several games were, for a number of
reasons. Gagne began to show the mixture of pitches that would
make him the league's strikeout leader. He began to show the
intelligence of a pitcher who knew how to combine the fastball
and the breaking ball. And he showed his background, attacking
the game with a hockey player's take-no-prisoners attitude.
Signed by the Dodgers out of Seminole Junior College in

Oklahoma, Gagne had grown up playing hockey in his hometown of Mascouche, Quebec.

In mid-April, the Missions were roughed up in El Paso, losing four of five games. Ill will between the teams grew when San Antonio pitchers—including Gagne—hit four Diablos players during the series. A week later, the teams were playing at Wolff Stadium in San Antonio, and Gagne was pitching. He brushed several El Paso hitters off the plate, including Julius Matos with a pitch high and inside. A couple of pitches later, Matos doubled, and he had words for Gagne as he stood at second base. Gagne's next pitch hit El Paso relief pitcher Brad Miadich on the top of the helmet, and Miadich charged the mound. Both dugouts emptied, and once order was restored, four Missions and five Diablos were ejected in the Texas League's first real brawl in four seasons. All the players involved were fined and suspended, but that didn't keep Gagne from continuing to pitch batters inside—and being successful. He was 4–1 with a 2.00 earned run average on June 1.

"It's just the way I pitch," Gagne told the *San Antonio Express-News* in July, when he was 8–2 with a 2.59 ERA and was selected for both the Double-A All-Star game and the Texas League All-Star game. "For some reason, El Paso thinks you shouldn't pitch inside. It's a man's game and that's how it's suppose to be played." He didn't knock anybody down in the Texas League All-Star game, but he did strike out four of the six batters he faced.

The next team to take offense at his aggressive style was Wichita, in a game at Wolff Stadium in August. Gagne hit the Wranglers' Emiliano Escandon in the helmet in the fifth inning, and in the sixth, Wichita pitcher Chad Durbin hit the Missions' Luke Allen. Allen and Durbin exchanged words, and Missions manager Jimmy Johnson ran onto the field to argue that Durbin had thrown at Allen. But Johnson was intercepted by Wranglers manager John Mizerock between the mound and the plate, and the managers tangled, causing the dugouts and bullpens to empty.

Once things had quieted down, of course, Gagne set everything off again. His pitching arm wrapped in ice, he stirred up the Wranglers with a rude arm gesture that ignited another melee.

Gagne's final start in San Antonio was on September 3. After five solid innings, pitching coach Mark Brewer told him he was out of the game. Gagne started to protest, but then Brewer told him the reason—he was being promoted to the major leagues. Gagne wound up leading the Texas League in strikeouts, 185 in 167⅔ innings, and ERA, at 2.63, and he was named the league's Pitcher of the Year. Four days after his promotion to the majors, Gagne made his big-league debut, starting for the Dodgers and giving up two hits and no runs in six innings against the Florida Marlins.

The Dodgers couldn't decide what to do with Gagne for the next two years, moving him between the starting rotation and the bullpen. But in the spring of 2002, without an established closer on the roster, they gave him the job. With his aggressive nature channeled into brief busts, Gagne responded with 52 saves, a 4–1 record, and a 1.97 ERA. In 2003, he won the National League Cy Young Award by converting on 55 of 55 save opportunities with an ERA of 1.20 and 137 strikeouts in 82⅓ innings. By then, everyone knew who the big kid from Quebec was.

=57=
THE EXPRESS

THE ROUND ROCK EXPRESS NEEDED A SPOT START LATE IN May of the 2000 season. What they got was an ace. Roy Oswalt, a skinny twenty-two-year-old kid from Mississippi, was called up from Kissimmee of the Class A Florida State League to make one start for the Express on May 25. He even came to the Dell Diamond in Round Rock with a round-trip airline ticket.

Pitching against the San Antonio Missions, Oswalt struggled a little in the first inning. He struck out the side in the second. He allowed a hit and a walk in the third, escaping without allowing a run, then struck out the next five Missions hitters in the fourth and fifth. He pitched out of his only serious problem of the night, getting a double-play ball with the bases loaded to end the seventh inning. When he was done, Oswalt had pitched a complete-game shutout and had fifteen strikeouts. And he was staying in Double-A.

But Oswalt wasn't the only big story in Round Rock in 2000. The team itself was a story. After years of failed attempts to bring the Austin area back into the Texas League—the capital had dropped out after the 1967 season—baseball was finally back. It took one of the biggest names in Texas sports to make it happen. Hall of Fame pitcher Nolan Ryan and his friend Don Sanders bought the Jackson Generals in 1998 and announced they were moving the team to Round Rock. The club would retain its long-standing relationship with the Houston Astros, making it even more of an attraction.

With help from Ryan, the central Texas suburb built a show-place of a stadium and got the community's biggest employer, computer maker Dell, to buy naming rights. Season-ticket sales were so brisk that the team cut off full-season packages at 4,500, and the Express sold 2,600 more fourteen-game packages. All twenty-three luxury suites sold in three weeks, with minimal marketing effort. The story of the Round Rock Express—named in part for the railroad line that runs just outside the park, but more for Nolan Ryan's nickname, the Ryan Express—was told in papers ranging from the *San Antonio Express-News* to *USA Today*.

A crowd of 10,669 packed the Dell Diamond on opening night. Ryan, whose son Reid was named president of the team, was in uniform that night and spoke to the team for more than an hour before the contest. Although the El Paso Diablos spoiled the show by winning 4–1, Round Rock was off and rolling. The Astros stocked the team with some of their best prospects, including hard-hitting second baseman Keith Ginter, who went 5 for 5 in the third game of the season in El Paso, then hit two home runs and drove in five a week later at Midland. On April 26, Eric Cole had three hits, including a grand slam, in a 12–2 victory at Tulsa. Two days before Oswalt arrived, third baseman Morgan Ensberg hit two three-run homers in a 9–3 romp over the Missions, and on June 3, he hit three homers and drove in eight runs in a victory over Shreveport. Round Rock powered through the first half of the schedule, earning a spot in the playoffs with a 43–27 record.

Attendance records kept falling, too. The Express drew 11,587 fans on July 4, moving into the top ten in single-season attendance in Texas League history—with thirty-three home games remaining. By the end of the second half, Round Rock's numbers were jaw-dropping. The Express had attracted 660,110 fans, crushing the Texas League record set by San Antonio in 1994 and the Double-A mark established by Nashville in 1980. The fans continued to come in the postseason—7,124 showed up for the West division opener against El Paso.

Round Rock lost the opener of the best-of-five series but came back in the next two games with strong starts by Wilfredo Rodriguez and Tim Redding to take a 2–1 lead. The Diablos won the next night to even the series, but in the eleventh inning of game five, Round Rock's Colin Porter hit a dramatic two-out solo home run for the victory.

The Express had to take two flights and a bus ride to reach Wichita, whose Wranglers had won the East playoffs the day before. The team arrived in Wichita at noon the day of the game but came out and beat the Wranglers 3–2, as Ginter and Kevin Burns hit home runs off Wichita ace Enrique Calero. The next night, Redding held the Wranglers to six hits and no earned runs, as the Express took a 9–3 victory. Wichita won game three, and the series moved to Round Rock.

A crowd of 11,325—the largest Texas League postseason crowd in fifty-four years—showed up for game four at the Dell Diamond, and Ginter came through again, launching a 425-foot, three-run homer in the bottom of the eighth for a 4–2 victory. The next night a crowd of 11,611, the biggest of the season, showed up to see the Express romp to the pennant, winning 8–4 behind four hits by Jhonny Perez. Ginter, the Texas League Player of the Year, and third baseman Ensberg were called up to the Astros after the game, while they were on the field celebrating the victory.

Manager Jackie Moore, the Texas League Manager of the Year, summed up both the game and the season: "Everybody that got us here is part of the victory tonight. Some of them aren't even here any more, but we wouldn't be celebrating this championship without the contributions they made." The contributors included Oswalt, who was 11–4 with a league-best 1.94 earned run average and 141 strikeouts; Ginter, who won the batting title at .333; and Cole, who led the league in doubles with 46.

Round Rock continued to prosper, breaking its own attendance records in each of the next four seasons. In 2003, Ryan and Sanders purchased a Triple-A team to bring to the Dell Diamond, with the Texas League team moving to a new downtown stadium in Corpus Christi in 2005.

=58=
ON A MISSION

SINCE JOINING WITH THE BRAND-NEW TEXAS LEAGUE OF Base Ball Clubs in the spring of 1888, San Antonio has endured far more heartaches than it has seen pennants. The Alamo City's club has suffered through many a long, hot summer of second-division baseball. San Antonio went through a fifteen-year drought after its 1933 pennant and thirty-three years after the 1964 club's championship.

Part of the blame has to go to the team's major-league affiliates, ranging from the hapless St. Louis Browns to the heartless Los Angeles Dodgers. For many years, player development was stressed over winning, especially during its twenty-four-year affiliation with the Los Angeles Dodgers. San Antonio saw a string of great young players during its time with the Dodgers—including Pedro Martinez, Mike Piazza, and Eric Karros—but just one championship.

So expectations were high in 2001 when San Antonio began its affiliation with the Seattle Mariners, and they were fulfilled—the Missions won the second half in the West Division, then fell to Round Rock in a dramatic five-game series.

But the next spring, it looked like the same old Missions. The club got off to an awful start—pitching well and getting no offense in some games or hitting well and getting no pitching in others—and finished the first half with a woeful 25–45 record, seventeen games behind first-place Round Rock.

The second half started out better, as the hitting and pitching started to improve. Some of the veteran leaders on the team like Andy Barkett began to take charge, and the Missions slowly began to win. They got a lift when the Mariners promoted their hottest young hitting prospect, Greg Dobbs, from Class A to San Antonio in July. Dobbs seemed to be the spark the Missions had needed. By the middle of August, they were ten games over .500, and they won nine of their last twelve games to claim the second half of the season.

San Antonio won the first game of the division playoff against Round Rock on Barkett's run-scoring single in the tenth, and the Missions went on to take the series.

The first game of the league championship series in Tulsa was one of the oddest in league history. San Antonio did not manage a hit against Drillers pitching for 9⅔ innings, but the Missions were still in the 2–2 game because of seven walks. In the tenth, Adrian Myers came up with San Antonio's only hit—a single that scored Antonio Perez with the winning run. The evenly matched teams battled all the way to game seven, which San Antonio won behind a dominating performance by starter Rafael Soriano, who allowed just two hits and struck out fifteen in seven innings.

The next spring, Dobbs came to San Antonio as the team's third baseman—and promptly tore his Achilles tendon, ending his season after two games in April. So backup Justin Leone, who had been a mediocre player in Class A, got the job. Leone proceeded to lead the Missions to one of the best seasons in San Antonio history.

The team's hard-hitting lineup—matched by a pitching staff that included three of the top four strikeout totals in the league and the league saves leader—helped San Antonio run away with both halves in the West. The 2003 Missions broke a San Antonio record (set in 1908) with an eighteen-game winning streak that took them from last to a runaway first during the first half of the season, then claimed the second half by seven games over Midland.

Leone was named the Texas League Player of the Year after tying for the league lead in doubles (38) and leading the league in extra-base hits (66), on-base percentage (.405), and runs scored (103). Travis Blackley was the league's Pitcher of the Year after winning a league-high seventeen games, and Dave Brundage was the Manager of the Year. It was the first sweep of all three honors ever for San Antonio.

The Missions beat Frisco four games to one for their second straight title. It was the first back-to-back playoff championships in San Antonio's ninety-eight years in the league.

CONCLUSION

IN OCTOBER 2003, AFTER FOUR SEASONS OF UNMATCHED attendance, the Texas League suffered a major loss when Nolan Ryan announced that his investment group had purchased a Triple-A team to play at the Dell Diamond. After five years in the league, Round Rock would be moving up, and the league would lose its best-drawing city.

But as has been the case in the last fifteen years, there was good news to offset the bad—Ryan's Double-A team would be moving to Corpus Christi, which has grown considerably since it was last in the league in the 1950s. Ryan's magic worked on the city by the bay just as it had in the Austin area, and local voters approved the financing and building of a new stadium after years of opposition. The downtown ballpark, which will open in spring 2005, will have a spectacular view of the Corpus Christi Bay and harbor as well as its towering harbor bridge.

There were times in the history of the league when losing a market with the size and the spending power of Austin–Round Rock would have been an enormous setback. But the fact that an owner would continue to keep the team—and put it in a new and fertile market—demonstrates the financial power of minor-league baseball, which continues to outperform the majors when it comes to the bottom line. And that financial power means the Texas League will continue to be strong and viable for years to come.

The league's makeup changed again following the 2004 season. The El Paso Diablos were sold, and the team was moved to the fast-growing market of Springfield, Missouri.

The moves to Corpus Christi and Springfield probably won't be the last in league history. There is a growing trend in the minors toward placing teams in large urban markets—like Frisco or Brooklyn—and being successful with them. Even with major-league teams in those markets, the minors have thrived on the inexpensive and fun-first nature of the minors. The trend means it's entirely possible that the Texas League could someday return to Fort Worth or Houston, as an alternative to, not a competitor with, the big leagues.

The biggest obstacles will be money and facilities. The days are long gone when a Double-A team could be purchased for tens of thousands of dollars and run one step ahead of the bill collectors. And the major-league affiliates will no longer allow their young prospects to play in anything but first-class, well-maintained ballparks. The days of El Paso's creaky Dudley Dome and San Antonio's scrounged-from-pieces V. J. Keefe Field have passed.

But no matter where the Texas League goes, it will continue to be a strong and vibrant part of the sports history of the state and the region, a backdrop to growth far into the twenty-first century.

POSTSCRIPT

At Tom's insistence, we're including this gem of a sports story, dated Sept. 8, 1919 from the Galveston Daily News. He originally discovered it while doing research on all the no-hitters in Texas League history and fell in love with the collection of odd adjectives—when was the last time you saw "funereal" and "dolorous" in a sports story—and enormous vocabulary—"ennui" in the crowd, runners "perigrinating" (speeding) around the bases and the umpire announcing the "cognomens" (names) of the teams—not to mention the powerful leadin that put you in the crowd, amid the back-to-back whippings of the hometown Galveston Pirates by the San Antonio Aces.

The writer's facility for the language and ability to put color to even the most commonplace of baseball moments makes the story special, as when the Pirates "died with their spikes on the initial cushion," meaning they never got a runner past first base. Of course, the subject was worthy—San Antonio's Fagan Burch, who was just 6-8 as a part-time pitcher in 1919, threw a no-hitter in the second game, and the fact that the last-place Aces could string together back-to-back shutouts was unusual in itself.

It took a bit of research, but it turned out that there was a reason the story about a late-season doubleheader in 1919 stood out.

The byline—Ed Angly—didn't offer many clues, but a search for the last name did.

In 1919, Angly was a 21-year-old veteran of World War I who had just graduated from the University of Texas. A decade later, known as Edward Angly, he was working for the Associated Press in Europe. And in 1939, as the London bureau chief for the New York Herald-Tribune—arguably the best newspaper in the country—he covered the British retreat out of Europe and was in the middle of the Battle of Britain, to the point of escaping death when a German bomb hit the Herald-Tribune office in London. Two years later, as the paper's Far East correspondent, he was one of the first U.S. writers to reach Pearl Harbor. He covered the war in the Pacific and in Europe on the front lines, and his last newspaper job was Paris bureau chief for the Chicago Sun.

He died in New York in 1951. But almost 50 years later, one of his first efforts in the newspaper business still stands out:

BURCH HOLDS CORSAIRS HITLESS AFTER BARFOOT WHITEWASHED THEM

By Ed Angly

In their last two battles on foreign terrain this year the San Antonio Aces covered themselves with glory and the Pirates with great gobs of whitewash before a crowd of 2,000 people, who conducted themselves with the same demeanor demanded by all rules of etiquette of those participating in the last rites over the body of a departed being. Save for the drowsy tinklings of pop bottles bumping together in the salesboys' tin containers and the crash of a Ford against an automobile outside the park, there was little to disturb the serene atmosphere. The grandstand seemed a crowded mourners' bench.

The funereal silence befitted the occasion. Ennui was perfectly excusable. With the exception of those who were paid for attending and scoring the battle, yawning and nodding were permissible. For the Pirates went to bat and back to the field without accomplishing anything through sixteen piteous innings. In the field, errors of omission and commission were frequent enough to give the Aces more runs than they deserved. As a result of all these tearful circumstances, the visitors made a clean weep of their four-game series, winning the Sunday opener by a 3-to-0 count and grabbing the farewell party with a 4-to-0 result.

Manager Fagan Burch of the invading baseball army personally conducted the final drive of his troopers around the four bases of operations. The Ace skipper turned loose a superb collection of outshoots, incurves and other varieties of heaves and kicked the pirates deeper into the cellar without even giving them a hit of any kind. Just four of the homelings got to first base during Burch's hitless seven-inning tenure of the mound. Three times Fagan B. walked a local batter, and once an infield error gave first base a Galveston occupant. None of the locals reached the midway station. All of them died with their spikes on the initial cushions.

That Fatal Fifth!

Following a precedent set during the first two clashes of the series the Aces put over their first Sunday victory with a cluster of hits in the fifth inning. Up to that time Bob Couchman had worked efficiently. He had been hit in every inning, but always when visitors were warming the hassocks Bob called on his reserve and got out of danger.

Ted Menze started the dolorous proceedings when he dropped Hub Northen's fly to the sun field as the fifth got under way. The swift-heeled Northen went to second before the ball could be returned to the zone of operations. Champlin bunted. The Pirates tried to force Northen at third, but he was going lickety-split and both men were securely implanted on the first and third corners.

Walgamot pushed his two perigrinating comrades over the counting rubber by smashing a two-base wallop to left field. The San Antonio receiver scored on Dunckel's single, completing one burst of offensive strength during the opening tussle.

Soldier Clybe Barfoot held the Pirates at bay throughout the first game. His offerings found the weak spots of the local batters except in six instances. The sextet of bingles were smeared over five innings, and Barfoot had little difficulty in wielding the whitewash brush.

Only once did the Pirates even threaten to score. That was in the fourth inning when Snedecor reached third and Clark got to second with two down. Hauser knocked n knocked a fly into right field, and Northen captured it after a long run. Hub tumbled over head first as he made the catch, but he had a bulldog grip on the ball and held it, retiring the side.

Although the visitors made their customary run in the fifth inning, the second game was bottled and labeled with San Antonio trademark in the first round. John Smithson and the rest of the local defense went completely to the eternal bow-wows shortly after Umpire Miller has cleared his throat and chirped out the cognomens of the two batteries.

Fireworks No. 2

Fuller took the center of the stage as the curtain went up and hammered a grounder to Buddy Ammons. Buddy threw the ball several feet inside first base and Snedecor dropped it in trying to touch the passing Ace. Dunckel sacrificed. Hale then knocked a long hit to left. Menze got the sphere on the bounce and pegged in to kill of Fuller at the plate. The ball landed on the back of Fuller's cerebellum just as he touched the rubber, knocking the Ace infielder cold for several minutes. Smithson then blew up higher than a kite and walked Jackson.

Hale and Jackson attempted a double steal and Dowle threw

the ball to left field on an attempt to stop Sammy at the hot corner. Hale came in home and Jackson went to third before the leather got back to the infield. Smithson walked Brown. Northen hit to Hauser and was out at first, Jackson scoring on the play. The left-hander followed this third catastrophe by hitting one of Champlin's ribs and Tarleton yanked his southpaw and sent Duffy to the first line of defense. Wagamont popped up and ended the protracted period of suffering.

Except in the fifth when Fuller singled and went to third when Dowie overthrew second to catch him stealing, and scored on Hale's sacrifice fly to Menze, the Aces were not at all unpleasant in their actions.

Nor did the Pirates cause any worry in the interior of the fifteen visiting craniums. Fagan Burch turned them back inning and inning without the least semblance of a hit. Duffy threatened to slap a single through third base once, but the superplayer yelept Sammy Hale stopped the hard drive.

APPENDIX

TEXAS LEAGUE PLAYERS OF THE YEAR

1931: Dizzy Dean, Houston
1932: Hank Greenberg, Beaumont
1933: Zeke Bonura, Dallas
1934: Charlie English, Galveston
1935: Rudy York, Beaumont
1936: Les Mallon, Dallas
1937: Ash Hillin, Oklahoma City
1938: Dizzy Trout, Beaumont
1939: Nick Cullop, Houston
1940: Bob Muncrief, San Antonio
1941: Rip Russell, Tulsa
1942: Dick Wakefield, Beaumont
1946: Hank Schenz, Tulsa
1947: Al Rosen, Oklahoma City
1948: Irv Noren, Fort Worth
1949: Herb Conyers, Oklahoma City
1950: Gil McDougald, Beaumont
1951: Jim Dyck, San Antonio
1952: Billy Hunter, Fort Worth

1953: Joe Frazier, Oklahoma City
1954: Frank Kellert, San Antonio
1955: Ray Murray, Dallas
1956: Ken Guettler, Shreveport
1957: Jim Frey, Tulsa
1958: Mike Lutz, Corpus Christi
1959: Carl Warwick, Victoria
1960: Chuck Hiller, Rio Grande Valley
1961: Phil Linz, Amarillo
1962: Cap Peterson, El Paso
1963: Jim Beauchamp, Tulsa
1964: Joe Morgan, San Antonio
1965: Leo Posada, Amarillo
1966: Tom Hutton, Albuquerque
1967: Nate Colbert, Amarillo
1968: Jim Spencer, El Paso; Bill Sudakis, Albuquerque (cowinners)

1969: Bobby Grich, Dallas–Fort Worth; Larry Johnson, Dallas–Fort Worth (cowinners)
1970: Mickey Rivers, El Paso
1971: Enos Cabell, Dallas–Fort Worth
1972: Randy Elliott, Alexandria
1973: Hector Cruz, Arkansas
1974: John Balaz, El Paso
1975: Gary Alexander, Lafayette
1976: Willie Aikens, El Paso
1977: Karl Pagel, Midland
1978: Bobby Clark, El Paso
1979: Mark Brouhard, El Paso
1980: Tim Leary, Jackson
1981: Steve Sax, San Antonio
1982: Darryl Strawberry, Jackson
1983: Mark Gillaspie, Beaumont
1984: James Steels, Beaumont
1985: Billy Jo Robidoux, El Paso

1986: Steve Stanicek, El Paso
1987: Gregg Jefferies, Jackson
1988: Jeff Manto, Midland
1989: Ray Lankford, Arkansas
1990: Henry Rodriguez, San Antonio
1991: John Jaha, El Paso
1992: Troy O'Leary, El Paso
1993: Roberto Petagine, Jackson
1994: Tim Unroe, El Paso
1995: Johnny Damon, Wichita
1996: Bubba Smith, Tulsa
1997: Mike Kinkade, El Paso
1998: Tyrone Horne, Arkansas
1999: Adam Piatt, Midland
2000: Keith Ginter, Round Rock
2001: Jason Lane, Round Rock
2002: Chad Tracy, El Paso
2003: Justin Leone, San Antonio
2004: Ryan Shealy, Tulsa

TEXAS LEAGUE PITCHERS OF THE YEAR

1933: George Darrow, Galveston
1934: Ash Hillin, San Antonio
1935–42: No Award Given
1946: Prince Oana, Dallas
1947: Clarence Beers, Houston
1948: Harry Perkowski, Tulsa
1949: Joe Landrum, Fort Worth
1950: Wayne McLeland, Dallas
1951: Bob Turley, San Antonio
1952: Hal Erickson, Dallas
1953: Don Fracchia, Beaumont
1954: John Andre, Shreveport

1955: Red Murff, Dallas
1956: Bert Thiel, Dallas
1957: Tommy Bowers, Dallas
1958: Joe Kotrany, Dallas
1959: Carroll Beringer, Victoria
1960: Jack Curtis, San Antonio
1961: Larry Maxie, Austin
1962: Gordie Richardson, Tulsa
1963: Camilo Estevis, Albuquerque
1964: Chris Zachary, San Antonio
1965: Ken Nixon, Austin

1966: Fred Norman, Dallas–Fort Worth

1967: John Duffie, Albuquerque

1968: Santiago Guzman, Arkansas

1969: Bill Frost, Amarillo

1970: Jim Flynn, Albuquerque

1971: Wayne Garland, Dallas–Fort Worth

1972: Dave Freisleben, Alexandria

1973: Frank Tanana, El Paso

1974: Randy Wiles, Arkansas (left-hander); Dennis Eckersley, San Antonio (right-hander) (cowinners)

1975–80: No Award Given

1981: Alan Fowlkes, Shreveport

1982: Jeff Bittiger, Jackson

1983: Sid Fernandez, San Antonio

1984: Calvin Schiraldi, Jackson

1985: Juan Nieves, El Paso

1986: George Ferran, Shreveport

1987: Dennis Cook, Shreveport

1988: Blaine Beatty, Jackson

1989: Andy Benes, Wichita

1990: Anthony Young, Jackson

1991: Paul McClellan, Shreveport

1992: Dan Smith, Tulsa

1993: Ben Van Ryn, San Antonio

1994: Sid Roberson, El Paso

1995: Steve Bourgeois, Shreveport

1996: Keith Foulke, Shreveport

1997: Steve Woodard, El Paso

1998: Jose Jimenez, Arkansas

1999: Eric Gagne, San Antonio

2000: Bud Smith, Arkansas

2001: Tim Redding, Round Rock

2002: Kirk Saarloos, Round Rock

2003: Travis Blackley, San Antonio

2004: Jeff Francis, Tulsa

TEXAS LEAGUE TEAM NAMES

Albuquerque	Dukes 1962–64; Dodgers 1965–71
Alexandria	Aces 1972–75
Amarillo	Gold Sox, 1959–63 and 1976–82; Sonics, 1965–67; Giants, 1968–74
Ardmore	Territorians, 1904; Rosebuds, 1961
Arkansas	Travelers, 1966–present
Austin	Senators, 1888–90, 1895–99, 1905, 1907–08, 1911–14 and 1956–64; Braves 1965–67
Beaumont	Oilers, 1912–17, 1919; Exporters, 1920–42, 1946–49 and 1953–55; Roughnecks, 1950–52; Golden Gators, 1983–86
Cleburne	Railroaders, 1906
Corpus Christi	Giants, 1958–59; Hooks, 2005–present

Corsicana	Oil City Indians, 1902; Oil Citys, 1902–04; Oilers, 1905
Dallas	Hams, 1888; Tigers, 1889–90; Hams, 1892; Steers, 1895 and 1923–38; Navigators, 1896; Defenders, 1897; Colts, 1898; Griffins, 1902; Giants, 1903–16 and 1922; Marines, 1919–22; Rebels, 1939–42 and 1946–48; Eagles, 1949–57; Rangers, 1958
Dallas–Fort Worth	Spurs, 1965–71
Denison	Indians, 1896
El Paso	Sun Kings, 1962–70 and 1973; Sun Dodgers, 1972; Diablos, 1974–2004
Fort Worth	Colts, 1897; Panthers, 1888–90, 1892, 1895–96 and 1902–32; Cats, 1933–42, 1946–58 and 1964
Frisco	RoughRiders, 2003–present
Galveston	Giants, 1888; Sand Crabs, 1889–90, 1892, 1895–99, 1907–12, and 1921–24; Pirates, 1912–17 and 1919–20; Buccaneers, 1931–37
Greenville	Hunters, 1906
Houston	Babies, 1888; Mud Cats 1889–90, 1892; Magnolias, 1895; Buffalos, 1896–99, 1907–42 and 1946–58
Jackson	Mets, 1975–90; Generals, 1991–99
Lafayette	Drillers, 1975–76
Longview	Cannibals, 1932
Memphis	Blues, 1968–73
Midland	Cubs, 1972–84; Angels, 1985–98; RockHounds, 1999–present
New Orleans	Pelicans, 1888
Oklahoma City	Indians, 1909, 1933–42, and 1946–57; Mets, 1910–11
Paris	Texas Midland Tigers, 1896; Texas Midlands, 1897; Parisians, Eisenfelder's Homeseekers, 1902; Steers, 1903; Red Ravens, 1904
Rio Grande Valley	Giants, 1960–61
Round Rock	Express, 2000–04
San Antonio	(?), 1888; Missionaries, 1892, 1895; Bronchos, 1896–97, 1899, and 1907–18; Gentlemen, 1898;

	Aces, 1919; Bears, 1920–28; Indians, 1929–32; Missions, 1933–42, 1946–62, 1968–71 and 1988–present; Bullets, 1963–64; Brewers, 1972–76; Dodgers, 1977–87;
Sherman	Orphans, 1895; Students, 1896
Sherman-Denison	Tigers, 1897; Students, 1902
Shreveport	Grays, 1895; Pirates, 1908–10; Gassers, 1915–24; Sports, 1925–32, 1938–42, and 1946–57; Braves, 1968–70; Captains, 1971–2000; Swamp Dragons, 2001–02
Springfield	Cardinals, 2005–present
Temple	Boll Weevils, 1905–07
Texarkana	Casket Makers, 1902
Tulsa	Oilers, 1933–42, and 1946–65; Drillers, 1977–present
Tyler	Sports, 1932
Victoria	Rosebuds, 1958–61; Giants, 1961; Toros, 1974
Waco	Babies, 1889; Indians, 1890; Central City, 1892; Tigers, 1897, 1902, and 1905; Steers, 1903; Navigators, 1906–19; Cubs, 1925–30
Wichita	Pilots, 1987–88; Wranglers, 1989–present
Wichita Falls	Spudders, 1920–32

TEXAS LEAGUE TEAMS' MAJOR-LEAGUE AFFILIATES

Albuquerque	Kansas City 1962; Los Angeles 1963–71
Alexandria	San Diego 1972–75
Amarillo	Baltimore 1959; New York (AL) 1960–62; Chicago (NL) 1963; Houston 1965–67; San Francisco 1968–74; San Diego 1976–82
Ardmore	Baltimore 1961
Arkansas	St. Louis 1966–2000; Anaheim 2001–present
Austin	Milwaukee 1956–65; Atlanta 1966–67
Beaumont	Detroit 1930–42; New York (AL) 1946–52; Chicago (NL) 1954; Milwaukee 1955; San Diego 1983–86

Corpus Christi	San Francisco 1958–59; Houston 2005–present
Dallas	Chicago (AL) 1935–38; Detroit 1946–47; Cleveland 1951–52; New York (NL) 1955–57
Dallas/Fort Worth	Chicago (NL) 1965–67; Houston 1968; Baltimore 1969–71
El Paso	San Francisco 1962–64; California 1965–70; Los Angeles 1972; California 1973–80; Milwaukee (AL) 1981–97; Milwaukee (NL) 1998; Arizona 1999–2004
Fort Worth	Detroit 1919–29; Cincinnati 1930–38; Brooklyn 1946–56; Brooklyn and Chicago (NL), 1957; Chicago (NL), 1958, 1964
Frisco	Texas 2003–present
Houston	St. Louis (NL) 1919–42, 1946–58
Jackson	New York (NL) 1975–90; Houston 1991–99
Lafayette	San Francisco 1975–76
Longview	St. Louis (AL) 1932
Memphis	New York (NL) 1968–73
Midland	Chicago (NL) 1972–84; California 1985–96; Anaheim 1997–98; Oakland 1999–present
Oklahoma City	Cleveland 1941; New York (NL) 1942; Cleveland 1946–50; Boston 1956–57
Rio Grande Valley	San Francisco 1960–61
Round Rock	Houston 2000–04
San Antonio	St. Louis (AL) 1933–42, 1946–53; Baltimore 1954–58; Chicago (NL) 1959–62; Houston 1963–64; Chicago (NL) 1968–71; Milwaukee 1972; Cleveland 1973–75; Texas 1976; Los Angeles 1977–2000; Seattle 2001–present
Shreveport	Philadelphia (AL) 1923–24; Chicago (AL) 1939, 1942, 1946; Atlanta 1968–70; California 1971–72; Milwaukee 1973–74; Pittsburgh 1975–78; San Francisco 1979–2002
Springfield	St. Louis, 2005–present
Tulsa	Pittsburgh 1933; Chicago (NL) 1940–42, 1946–47; Cincinnati 1948–54; Cleveland 1955; Chicago (NL) 1956; Philadelphia 1957–58; St. Louis

1959–65; Texas 1977–2002; Colorado 2003–
present

Victoria   Los Angeles 1958–59; Detroit 1960; Baltimore
1961; San Francisco 1961; New York (NL) 1974

Wichita   San Diego 1987–94; Kansas City 1995–present

Wichita Falls   Pittsburgh 1920–21; Chicago (NL) 1922–25; St.
Louis (AL) 1928–32

TEXAS LEAGUE BALLPARKS SINCE 1920

Albuquerque   Tingley Field 1962–68; Albuquerque Sports
Stadium 1969–71

Alexandria   Bringhurst Field 1972–75

Amarillo   Potter County Memorial Stadium 1959–63,
1965–74, 1976–82

Ardmore   Cardinal Park 1961

Arkansas   Travelers Field 1966; Ray Winder Field 1966–
present

Austin   Disch Field 1956–67

Beaumont   Magnolia Ballpark 1920–28; Stuart Stadium 1929–
42, 1946–55; Vincent-Beck Stadium 1983–86

Corpus Christi   Cabanis Field 1958–59; Whataburger Field,
2005–present

Dallas   Joe Gardner Park 1920–24; Riverside Park 1924;
State Fair Racetrack 1924; Steers Stadium 1925–
38; Rebels Field 1939–42; Rebels Stadium 1946–
48; Burnett Field 1949–58

Dallas/Fort Worth   Turnpike Stadium 1965–71

El Paso   Dudley Field 1926–70, 1972–90; Cohen Stadium
1990–2004

Fort Worth   Panther Park 1920–28; LaGrave Field 1929–42,
1946–58, 1964

Frisco   Dr Pepper/Seven-Up Ballpark 2003–present

Galveston   Gulfview Park 1920–24; Moody Stadium 1931–
37

Houston   West End Park 1920–27; Buffalo Stadium 1928–
42, 1946–52; Busch Stadium 1953–58

Jackson	Smith-Wills Stadium 1975–99
Lafayette	Clark Field 1975–76
Longview	(?) 1932
Memphis	Blues Stadium 1968–73
Midland	Cubs Stadium 1972–84; Angels Stadium 1985–94; Max H. Christensen Stadium 1994–2001; First American Bank Ballpark 2002–present
Oklahoma City	Holland Field 1933–42, 1946–48; Texas League Park 1949–57
Rio Grande Valley	Giants Field 1960–61
Round Rock	The Dell Diamond 2000–04
San Antonio	League Park 1920–32; Eagle Field 1932; Tech Field 1932–42, 1946; Mission Stadium 1947–64; V. J. Keefe Memorial Stadium 1968–93; Municipal Stadium 1994–95; Nelson W. Wolff Municipal Stadium 1995–present
Shreveport	Gasser Park 1920–24; Sports Park 1925–32; Texas League Park 1938–42, 1946–57; Bonneau Peters Field 1968; Braves Field 1968–70; SPAR Stadium 1971–85; Fair Grounds Field 1986–2002
Springfield	John Q. Hammons Field, 2005–present
Tulsa	Tulsa Fairgrounds Grandstand 1933–33; Texas County Stadium, 1934; Texas League Park 1935–42, 1946–60; Oiler Park 1961–65; Driller Park 1977–80; Robert B. Sutton Stadium 1981–82; Tulsa County Stadium 1983–88; Drillers Stadium 1989–present
Tyler	Fair Park, 1932
Victoria	Riverside Park 1958–61; Toros Stadium 1974
Waco	Katy Park 1925–30
Wichita	Lawrence-Dumont Stadium 1987–present
Wichita Falls	Athletic Park 1920–32

ATTENDANCE RECORDS

Single-season league attendance record:	2,767,854, in 2003
Single-date attendance record:	54,151, Dallas, April 11, 1950

1. 2004 Round Rock, 689,286
2. 2003 Round Rock, 685,973
3. 2002 Round Rock, 670,176
4. 2001 Round Rock, 668,792
5. 2003 Frisco, 666,977

Arkansas: 296,428, in 1989
Corpus Christi: 87,774, in 1958
Frisco: 666,977, in 2003
Midland: 276,380, in 2002
San Antonio: 411,959, in 1994
Springfield: Begins play in 2005
Tulsa: 351,929, in 1999
Wichita: 236,378, in 1993

WIN–LOSS RECORDS

Arkansas: 30–18
Corpus Christi: 8–4
Frisco: 11–5
Midland: 7–14
San Antonio: 92–96
Springfield: Begins play in 2005
Tulsa: 97–98
Wichita: 36–39

Arkansas: 2,619–2,701
Corpus Christi: 143–154
Frisco: 154–126
Midland: 2,186–2,318
San Antonio: 6,768–7,063
Springfield: Begins play in 2005
Tulsa: 4,230–4,157
Wichita: 1,275–1,197

RECORDS FOR WINS AND LOSSES

Most Championships Won: Houston, 24
Most games won in a season: Fort Worth, 109, in 1922 and 1924
Fewest games won in a season: Paris-Ardmore, 27, in 1904
Longest winning streak: Corsicana, 27, in 1902
Most games lost in a season: Austin, 114, in 1914
Fewest games lost in a season: Corsicana, 23, in 1902
Longest losing streak: Austin, 32, in 1914

TEXAS LEAGUE CHAMPIONSHIPS FOR CURRENT TEAMS AS OF 2005

Arkansas (5):	1977, 1979, 1980, 1989, 2001
Corpus Christi (1)	1958
Frisco (1)	2004
Midland (1)	1975
San Antonio (10)	1897, 1903 (South Texas League), 1908, 1933, 1950, 1961, 1964, 1997, 2002, 2003
Springfield (0)	
Tulsa (8)	1936, 1949, 1960, 1962, 1963, 1982, 1988, 1998
Wichita (3)	1987, 1992, 1999

TEAM HITTING RECORDS

Most hits in a game:	53, Corsicana, June 15, 1902
Most runs in a game:	51, Corsicana, June 15, 1902
Most singles in a game:	26, Corsicana, June 15, 1902
Most doubles in a game:	13, Fort Worth, July 30, 1897
Most triples in a game:	6, Several teams
Most home runs in a game:	21, Corsicana, June 15, 1902

INDIVIDUAL HITTING RECORDS

Highest batting average:	.444, Algie McBride, Austin, 1895
Longest hitting streak:	37, Bobby Trevino, El Paso, 1969
Most hits in a season:	245, Randy Moore, Dallas, 1929
Most singles in a season:	187, Randy Moore, Dallas, 1929
Most doubles in a season:	70, Rhino Williams, Dallas, 1925
Most triples in a season:	30, Eddie Moore, Fort Worth, 1929
Most home runs in a season:	62, Ken Guettler, Shreveport, 1956
Most RBIs in a season:	196, Clarence Kraft, Fort Worth, 1924
Most hits in a game:	8, Several players
Most singles in a game:	7, Ollie Pickering, Houston, May 21, 1892; and Jim Paciorek, El Paso, April 30, 1983

Most doubles in a game: 5, Les Bell, Houston, May 28, 1923
Most triples in a game: 3, Several players
Most home runs in a game: 8, Jay "Nig" Clarke, Corsicana, June 15, 1902
Most RBIs in a game: 16, Jay "Nig" Clarke, Corsicana, June 15, 1902
Most stolen bases in a season: 146, Herman Bader, Dallas, 1889
Most stolen bases in a game: 6, John Frierson, Houston, July 26, 1914

INDIVIDUAL PITCHING RECORDS

Most innings pitched: 385, Lucky Wright, Corsicana, 1902
Most consecutive shutout   42, Tom Gorman, Beaumont, 1951
  innings:
Lowest ERA: 0.70, Frank Hoffman, Austin–San Antonio,
                               1888
Most wins: 35, Lucky Wright, Corsicana, 1902
Most consecutive wins: 19, Snipe Conley, Dallas, 1917
Most losses: 28, Bill Doyle, Temple, 1907
Most consecutive losses: 16, Floyd Kroh, Houston–Galveston–
                               Shreveport, 1920, and Bill Bailey, Houston,
                               1923
Most strikeouts in a season: 310, Harry Ables, San Antonio, 1910
Most walks in a season: 185, Bill Bailey, Beaumont, 1919
Most strikeouts in a game: 21, Dave Righetti, Tulsa, July 16, 1978
  (9 innings)
Most strikeouts in a game: 22, Bob Turley, San Antonio, August 11,
  (extra innings)   1951
Most walks in a game: 16, Rex Barney, Fort Worth, May 13, 1951

TEXAS-LEAGUERS
IN THE BASEBALL HALL OF FAME

Grover C. Alexander, pitcher: Dallas, 1930
Walter Alston, manager: Houston, 1937 (first baseman)
Sparky Anderson, manager: Fort Worth, 1955 (second baseman)
Jim Bottomley, first baseman: Houston, 1921

Steve Carlton, pitcher:	Tulsa, 1964
Dizzy Dean, pitcher:	Houston 1930–31; Tulsa, 1940
Dennis Eckersley, pitcher:	San Antonio, 1974
Hank Greenberg, first baseman:	Beaumont, 1931–32
Burleigh Grimes, pitcher:	Galveston, 1937
Chick Hafey, outfielder:	Houston, 1924
Rogers Hornsby, second baseman:	Oklahoma City, 1940–41 (manager); Fort Worth, 1942 (manager); Beaumont, 1950 (manager)
Carl Hubbell, pitcher:	Fort Worth, 1927; Beaumont, 1928
Willie McCovey, first baseman:	Dallas, 1957
Joe Medwick, outfielder:	Houston, 1931–32, 1948
Joe Morgan, second baseman:	San Antonio, 1964
Hal Newhouser, pitcher:	Beaumont, 1939
Phil Niekro, pitcher:	Austin, 1961
Gaylord Perry, pitcher:	Corpus Christi, 1959; Rio Grande Valley, 1960
Branch Rickey, executive:	Dallas 1904–05 (catcher)
Brooks Robinson, third baseman:	San Antonio 1956–57
Frank Robinson, outfielder:	Tulsa, 1954
Nolan Ryan, pitcher:	Round Rock, 2000–04 (owner); Corpus Christi, 2005–present (owner)
Al Simmons, outfielder:	Shreveport, 1923
George Sisler, first baseman:	Shreveport-Tyler, 1932 (first baseman, manager)
Duke Snider, outfielder:	Fort Worth, 1946; Albuquerque, 1967 (manager); Alexandria, 1972 (manager)
Tris Speaker, outfielder:	Cleburne, 1906; Houston, 1907
Don Sutton, pitcher:	Albuquerque, 1965
Bill Terry, first baseman:	Shreveport, 1916–17 (pitcher, outfielder
Earl Weaver, manager:	Houston 1951–52 (second baseman)
Zack Wheat, outfielder:	Shreveport, 1908
Billy Williams, outfielder:	San Antonio, 1959
Ross Youngs, outfielder:	San Antonio, 1913; Austin, 1914

TEXAS LEAGUE HALL OF FAME MEMBERS

Founders:	John J. McCloskey, Mike O'Connor, J. Doak Roberts
Executives:	Dick Burnett, J. Alvin Gardner, Paul LaGrave, Jim Paul, William Ruggles, Bill Valentine
Executive/player/manager:	Bobby Bragan
Umpire:	Wilson Mathews
Manager:	Jake Atz
Players:	Russ Burns, Paul Easterling, Ed Knoblauch, Clarence "Big Boy" Kraft, Pat Newnam, Homer Peel, Bobby Stow, Arch Tanner
Pitchers:	Joe Pate, Paul Wachtel
Pitcher/umpire:	Milt Steengrafe
Player/pitcher:	Dode Criss
Single-season/short career:	Ike Boone, Ken Guettler, Dave Hoskins, Red Murff, Howie Pollet

FORMER TEXAS LEAGUE PLAYERS
IN THE NATIONAL BASEBALL HALL OF FAME

Dizzy Dean
Hank Greenberg
Chick Hafey
Willie McCovey
Joe Medwick
Joe Morgan

Brooks Robinson
Al Simmons
Tris Speaker
Don Sutton
Billy Williams

For a complete list of sources and further reading,
please go to www.texasleague.com/history/research/

INDEX